Slavery and Soul

Ascended Master Djehuty
Channeled by Tom Jacobs

For you and me, for all of us.

ISBN-13: 978-1537403090
ISBN-10: 1537403095

OPENING...6

FOUR TRUTHS 8

ENERGETIC INHERITANCE 24

    KARMIC INHERITANCE.. 24
    ANCESTRAL INHERITANCE 46

DEHUMANIZATION 53

MULTIDIMENSIONALITY AND POWER........ 60

    OWNING YOUR CREATION 68

DEHUMANIZATION REVISITED 70

PERSPECTIVES 78

    SLAVERS... 78
    SLAVES... 81

VICTIMIZATION 84

    DISCONNECTION.. 98
    IDENTITY 105

RESOLVING AND RELEASING THE EFFECTS OF
SLAVERY...112

    ON HEALING 112
    STRATEGIES FOR RESOLUTION AND RELEASE 118
        Rewriting Your History 119
        Releasing the Energies of Others 123
        Calling Back Your Energy 127

CLOSING 130

MEDITATION: CLEARING ANCESTRAL AND
INDIVIDUAL KARMA 132

ABOUT DJEHUTY 143

ABOUT THE CHANNEL..143

Opening

The single truth that All That Is knows outside its human lives is that love is power. The truth that soul aims for its human selves to learn about this is that knowing, owning, and accepting all parts of yourself leads to real power, the power of love.

Manifesting the power of love is accomplished by an individual through dealing with emotions, thoughts, and other imprints gained over the course of many lives. This means living through and reliving all manner of experiences happy and unhappy, positive and negative. From the soul's perspective, it is absolutely mandatory that pleasurable as well as painful experiences are had by its human selves over the course of many lives. To believe that soul, God/Goddess, the Universe, or your higher self is going to protect you and/or wants you to be happy is naïve. The fact is that soul – as a portion of All That Is – requires that you become well-rounded when it comes to human experience, and all-knowing and all-accepting when it comes to who you are, what you feel, and what you are capable of being and doing. The expectation you may carry that life is or should be about safety is not grounds for criticizing you. It is, in fact, a reflection of the long-term journey of the evolution of consciousness that every being on the planet is undergoing. Now you are ready to grow beyond such expectations and step into true spiritual power, seeing your life as your soul – the portion of All That Is that you are – designed it.

Over the course of many millennia, All That Is experiences this arduous path of absolute and total self-knowledge and -acceptance through projecting the possession of power upon circumstances and situations in the external world. In fact, all energies that exist in the Universe are present within each and every human, and the process of self-knowledge and self-acceptance is enough to become truly powerful enough to inhabit your Divine nature while embodied as a human. But you have been conditioned to play externally focused games in order to find out who gets to have power when. *You do this until you learn about the true nature of power as love, acceptance, and compassion toward self, which naturally then flows from you toward others.*

When you truly and fully know yourself on all levels, you accept that all possibilities exist within you. When you recognize this and love yourself – warts and all – you hold space for the complexity of consciousness that you are as an expression of your soul. And when you know, accept, and love all of yourself, you are living as the Divine, connected with the wisdom of your soul.

Four Truths

The first truth you must accept if you are to truly understand the dynamics of slaver and your human history on both sides of it over time: *Slavery exists on all parts of the Earth timeline.* It reflects one angle of the critical need of All That Is to explore power dynamics while in human form.

Slavery, the owning and using of people, is an expression of the core motivation that creates the power based games humanity has been cycling through for as long as it has existed. You at times believe you are separate from Divine Source – All That Is – and you seek to explore the myriad ways you can come to perceive that you are powerful. Otherwise, you may see yourselves as helpless victims born to suffer and, at some point, die. It's not a fun picture to live with that in your mind and heart, so you try to make yourselves feel better through the externally directed games that bring and take away what your minds believe power to be.

It will be obvious to many of you in these games that through them you are seeking to be strong, but you need to see that you are predominantly defining strength as something that can be derived only from external sources. When you receive through the externally projected games what you consider to be power, you will do anything to hold onto it and make sure that no one can take it from you. In this state, you often live in perpetual fear that it can and will be taken away. The fact is that the money may go, youth will fade, others will tire of the charm or attractiveness you believe will keep you likeable and safe, and you will, at some point, die. You may live this way for many lifetimes without gaining conscious awareness of the cost of living in and from this fear, living your life as you tend to do with no thought to the vibrations you generate and live by.

If you were connected to self-love through absolute, unflinching self-knowledge and self-acceptance, you would inhabit your Divine power as a portion of All That Is. You would cease seeking to latch onto and grabbing for external images of what you think power is supposed to be and look like.

If you were thus connected, the hole inside you – the sense of lacking Divine love because you are separated from it and seem to be alone as you live and age on your way to a certain death – would be filled with self-awareness and acceptance. You would note the normal human tendency to assume that power comes from external sources, and you would love that part of your human nature. You would love it because it evidences your portion of All That Is, Divine Intelligence, or Source as it learns to go from fear into love, which is the purpose of each of your human lives on Earth. You would playfully catch various parts of yourself focused on external power in repeating their beliefs that power comes from doing, having, taking, overpowering, or killing something or someone. You would also be the source of love for yourself, aligning your conscious human self with your Divine self, your soul.

The second truth you must accept: *All souls involved in slavery are Divine beings agreeing to explore this kind of externally based power dynamic together.* Nothing of import can happen to a human without all of the souls involved engaged in a mutually-loving conspiracy behind the scenes. This includes all wonderful and awful experiences, all celebrations and all traumas. Every important life dynamic and experience of a human reflects and brings to life the themes the involved souls are living out while human. Each soul does this in order to learn what it means to be human, given a wide variety of variables. Each of us does so over the course of many lives spread out across the Earth timeline in order to have access to all the kinds of variables available to humans. *Souls don't incarnate on Earth only to be happy, and your soul's ideal for you has nothing to do with life, the world, or others being required to keep you safe and reassure you things are alright.*

Souls, as portions of All That is, already know what happiness and love are all about. Happiness stemming from generous love and acceptance of all things and all beings is the normal, natural state of all souls! We come here to live as humans to explore what it's like to be here and, ultimately, to get back to that loving state *while embodied.* Along the way, we naturally have all manner of frightening, painful, and frustrating challenges just as we naturally have experiences based in happiness, joy, creativity, and other wonderful energies.

In the predominant way of thinking about slavery on Earth, there are oppressors and victims. I call this overall mindset humanity has developed the victim/perpetrator paradigm. Your human mind cannot force its powerful logic into any other sort of notion, whether you feel sorry for the victims or not and hate the oppressors or not. In your schema of how it goes down, certain kinds of people are kidnapped, stolen, sold, or captured from home, village, or military situation and forced into servitude of one kind or another. These are the kinds of situations that can make it difficult for some of you to believe in a loving god, by the way, because your powerful logic of mind cannot reconcile the image of a loving god with this kind of obviously awful thing that individuals, communities, and tribal groups experience. "If God exists," you ask, "how could we do these things to each other? How could he let these things happen?" But you must consider what god you think is in charge of things! Each and every human is a portion of Divine Consciousness, also known as All That Is, and therefore is a god – a piece of what you term God. There is no external power doing these things or failing to do its job and letting suffering result – you are it. And All That Is is learning through your and all other humans' experiences what owning and using other humans is like and costs, and what it's like and costs to be someone who is owned by another.

I charge you to get grounded and become willing to see all the things that people do to each other as reflections of souls' agreements with other souls to learn everything they can through the lens of the myriad possible human experiences. When you can truly do this and still love yourself and others, you will be stepping into a mature experience of yourself as a portion of the Divine. Then you can see that certain themes *will* manifest in your life and how it is that you can and do, in fact, have choice in how that process happens and how you respond to what is in your life. In this mode, you will be able to see all that happens to you and others as serving your Divine mission, and you will see how to effortlessly and freely give others the benefit of the doubt, ending victim/perpetrator perceptions that are currently draining you of your Divine power. Yes, deciding that you and others are wrapped up in an inescapable victim/perpetrator situation leaks your energy. Adopting this worldview causes you to lose energy, which is power, in the face of what has hurt you. My mission in all of my teaching is to support you in coming out of disempowering perceptions and attitudes so you can step into your Divine power as a soul living life as a human. But only you can decide to do so and step into your power as a Divine being living a human life.

Ceasing to see through the victim/perpetrator lens is crucial to human evolution now. What stands in the way of letting it go for many may be a sense of overwhelm from the pain, suffering, and sorrow that you have known and carried for many lifetimes. These feelings can seem too awful suddenly to make meaningless by choosing to take some form of responsibility for what has happened. You have come to identify as what has hurt you, what has happened to you against your (conscious) will. Now your main job is to learn to deal with the stored emotions that have become built up in your energetic field. This is a large topic I explore in other texts and materials offered through this channel.[1] For our purposes in this text, understand that the primary route to your evolution during this time is learn to effectively deal with emotions still with you from the past as well as to learn to manage your feeling nature now.

---

[1] The first five channeled books from this channel: *Approaching Love*, *Understanding Loss and Death*, *Goddess Past, Present, and Future*, *Conscious Revolution: Tools for 2012 and Beyond*, and *Conscious Living, Conscious Dying*. The first four are collected in the volume *Djehuty Speaks*.

As a Divine being, each time you perceive something happens to you, you miss an opportunity to own the power that you do have. As a soul which is a portion of All That Is, your various levels of consciousness are vibrating energies that are, in effect, Divine commands. This is the nature of karma, which are beliefs tied to emotions: You assign meaning to why in a given situation you were hurt or helped, hated or loved, and that meaning can become entrenched in your consciousness to the point of vibrating nonstop and, as a result, creating your 3D reality around you. You will want to believe the 3D things happening around you as true and real because 3D seems real to you, and so you accept the manifestations of these pained or joyous beliefs in the material world as true. When this happens, things get cemented in your energy field/consciousness and, therefore, your life. But they are not true, they are manifest: They are happening because you are vibrating them into existence.[2]

Given this, if you believe that a painful thing has been done to you, you are giving power to the mani-

_____

[2] This will be explained in more detail in the next section on Energetic Inheritance.

festation of what you have vibrated. *You must instead own what has manifested in 3D in your life as the concretizing of something vibrating in your energetic field or in some level of consciousness (including the unconscious). You must assume that you have vibrated every single thing you have ever experienced into manifestation.* When you can do this with acceptance, graciousness, gratitude, and love, then you are no longer playing at and becoming a victim, and the true power of your Divine self as a loving being can become available to you.

Above, I mentioned that you develop identities surrounding what has happened to you. If you believe that you are your past and what you have experienced, it becomes easy to succumb to an error in logic through using the wrong kind of logic. Your human logic (that of your linear, logical mind) cannot grasp the logic of your soul, which is that of the Divine. I challenge you to begin identifying instead as a Divine being who is a work in progress, learning through making choices and dealing with the consequences, vibrating all you experience into manifestation so that you can learn to go from vibrating fear into vibrating love. This is what your soul is here to do, and so it is imperative that you learn it. At some point you will, but you alone will decide how much

16

suffering you're willing to endure by living through a lens of powerless, one in which things happen to you and you're the hapless victim of circumstance or the wills of others.

Slavery is one of the realities on your planet that inspires a tremendous amount of pain in large groups of people across the centuries. This pain can run so deep that most are not sure how to let it into consciousness, let alone heal it. Anger is a most common response to pain, and I encourage you to commit to viewing and interpreting all anger as a response to – and, ultimately, covering over or masking – pain. This will help you see how to be less distracted by the fire and drama of anger so that you can get through to the pain behind it. You have the option to feel less on the defensive when anger is present in the world around you or in yourself so that something productive can come out of the experience of feeling it. As I have elucidated elsewhere,[3] all of your soul's lives' records are in your emotional body now. If you respond to the reality of slavery with anger, this is okay. Know that this is natural because you have experienced slavery from both sides of the story

---

[3] *Conscious Revolution: Tools for 2012 and Beyond.* Available as a stand-alone volume and included in *Djehuty Speaks.*

at various junctures on the Earth timeline. But please be committed to remembering that remaining angry will not let you get to the source of the pain, which is of deep disempowerment, the deepest sense of powerlessness that humans can carry and feel. *Please decide that you are stronger than this anger and pain because you can choose to generate love through compassionate acceptance and gratitude.* Some life situations – and this definitely includes slavery – are harder nuts to crack by getting back to love, but the process results in the most rewarding experience any human can have: Reuniting with the Divine within through choosing to align with and embody Divine love.

The rationale for slavery in any given time and place is economic, one of the many arenas onto which humans have externally projected dreams of gaining and holding power. The criteria that in a given time and place define what kind of people are enslaved will vary. Skin color, ethnic heritage, tribal identity, geographical relationships, competition for resources, religion, gender, economic or immigration status, and other variables can come into play in different situations. Realize that any of these rationales for making others slaves in a given time and place is part of the experiment of All That Is to learn about what true power is. Any time a set of humans encounters a new set of others, there is the opportunity to respond to them with welcomeness or with fear. Sometimes it's a mixture of the two, and there are many times when groups meeting each other for the first time succeed in giving each other the benefit of the doubt and creating a positive shared experience together. Many of you have felt over time separated from Source, from Divine Love. As you coalesce around identifying features or shared ancestry of your own people, many groups of humans all over the timeline have developed an "us versus them" attitude – a tribal identity that leads to the group shielding and protecting itself from others, making others wrong for being different, and making up stories about others to make one's community feel better about itself and worse about the others.

It is true that in many of your soul's lives you were taught to fear and fight those other people who are different from you. Humans across time have feared that there is not enough for all, and the truth is that material reality functions in response to the energetic flow within you, as I have mentioned above and will describe in detail in the next section. You have, therefore, worried at times for your survival and viewed others as threats to it. This worry has created scenarios in which it seems to become true that there is not enough because if you think, feel, and believe it, it will come true in 3D around you.

For much of human history, it has been difficult for ethnic, religious, and other kinds of groups not to feel or perceive they are in competition for resources of all kinds with other groups. Cooperation among different groups certainly has happened and does happen, but I want to focus on what has gone on when it has not. If you are to heal the reality of the slavery that exists all across the Earth timeline and, in fact, still lives within your energetic fields now, you need to understand and see clearly the kinds of logics and rationales for assuming that people and groups different from you are somehow less than human. This topic cuts deeply for many.

A third truth that must be understood to fully grasp this topic and to heal millennia of oppression and pain surrounding the global reality of slavery: *Each and every one of you has, at some point along the Earth timeline, been a slave.* There is not one among you wonderful souls having temporary human trips who has chosen to avoid being owned by and put to work in some way by others. Whether it is because of a debt, skin color, religion, marriage, being a prisoner of war, or any other reason, you have all been through it. Not all of you right this minute feel the memory of that kind of way of life because not all of you need in the moment of this particular human life to process it. But it's there. All of you have been in that situation in various lives. All of you have been slaves. It is a natural and normal part of the process of each portion of All That Is (each soul) to experience it. It's part of being on Earth as a human, and every single soul is incarnating on Earth in a variety of lives in order to go through all that humans can go through, including disempowering realities such as slavery.

The fourth truth: *Each and every one of you has, at some point along the Earth timeline, owned slaves.* This is not something that not many would want to admit into conscious awareness, let alone own as a truth. But it is one, and you need to admit and own it. The kinds of power imbalances inherent in slavery, the injustice and oppression, are woven into the intentions of All That Is to learn about life as humans given different variables in various lives. All the different possible scenarios humans go through have been lived by each of you on all sides. This is the way that All That Is learns. Remember that Divine Source does not play victim/perpetrator games outside human life, and they do not identify as victims or perpetrators. Your soul and the souls of all others are engaged in loving discourse, weaving agreements and contracts based in love to help each other evolve while embodied as humans.

From the soul's point of view, there is only a slight difference between being owned as a human and owning other humans. Those on both sides of the ownership equation are learning a lesson All That Is becomes human to learn: What power is, where it comes from, who gets to have it when and why, and who can take it from whom when. Souls on either side of the ownership game of slavery are exploring together what it feels like to live through a power imbalance together, and it is a profoundly important path to walk together. It might not be obvious to all, but there are deep bonds on the human level that can form between abuser and abused, rapist and raped, owner and slave. The charged dynamics between humans working through such intense karmic individual and collective soul-educating experiences are some of the most intense available for humans to experience. Always you must remember that there are souls behind the scenes, and that these souls are entangled in a Divine conspiracy of love to provide each other myriad opportunities to, while temporarily in human form, go into and be in fear and transform out of into love.

Energetic Inheritance

Karmic Inheritance

For you to truly understand what I aim to get through to you in this teaching, you must understand karma from my point of view. Following this overview, I will explain what it means to carry and live with karma, and how to work with it in order to resolve it and move on with your life.

If you carry forward old conceptions of karma taught to you by your religions, you can easily fall into the trap of endlessly repeating the unhappy, destructive, and life-negating effects of your karma. If you believe these old stories, you will certainly define yourself and your life history in terms of the classic victim/perpetrator paradigm that at some point and to some degree has painfully mucked up every human life thus far. *That this teaching is coming through this channel now means that you are opening a door with your hearts to overcome the painful dynamics your mind has created in order to attempt to protect you from the pain that is an inevitable part of human life.* You cannot escape pain brought on by unhealthy power over/power under dynamics as described above. And you are ready to evolve beyond limiting conceptions of what is happening on Earth, what it means to make choices and deal with the results, and what it means that you have at times in your life experienced heavy and damaging difficulty and pain. That you cannot escape pain and hardship is a fact. If my heartfelt message for you contained in this text has found you, then you are at a place in your evolutionary journey at which you're ready to move beyond the fearful impulse to shut down, hide, and isolate that naturally grows from the victim/perpetrator karmic model of life on Earth that you have carried for so long.

You have been taught at times that karma is a system of reward and punishment. At other times, you've been taught that it's all about cause and effect, some kind of cosmic rule that "what goes around comes around." These conceptions inspired by your religions sort of, kind of, maybe somewhat in a way approach some snippet of the truth, but let me set the record straight for you so that you can proceed and take in my teachings on slavery and how to heal it from an appropriate mindset that will enable you to actually heal it. There's no need for you to remain stuck on a karmic hamster wheel that is, in fact, only a life force sapping construction of the human linear, logical mind to try to explain why pain, fear, disappointment, and loss feel so much like punishments of an angry god or cosmos.

You are not rewarded by anything in the entirety of the cosmos other than your (Divine) willingness to give and receive love.

You are not punished by anything in the entirety of the cosmos other than your (Divine) willingness to judge self and other, which is a way of withholding love from self and other.

There is no gold star/demerit system that holds you accountable for what you do and don't do, or can't help but do or refuse to do. Please permanently disavow all such conceptions of karma you've learned that may make you fear what could happen to you next, or instill in you a fear that you should be good now so you don't reap punishment later. It is all horse shit and needs to be edited out of the human learning process once and for all. Be aware of the times in your life when you might have done something that looks good, right, and/or noble for fear-based reasons, such as when you didn't assert a boundary or take care of yourself because someone else needed something and you didn't want to mess with your karma by saying "no" to someone. Always check the vibrations of your motivations and weed out those based in fear, even when they look like love. The motivations for your actions are always more important energetically – and therefore evolutionarily – than the actions themselves. As you evolve, you are learning to make better, more informed and conscious, more faith- and love-based choices, which is what your soul has you here to do.

The basic fact about karma is that it comprises your beliefs about why things happen. A belief is formed after something important happens to you, whether happy or sad, joyful or painful, or empowering or disempowering. You could think of it a mind-centered imprint associated with and attached to a moment, process, or event that deeply impacts you. In other words, something happens that affects you energetically and emotionally in an important way. Your mind then ascribes a reason to why it happened, doing the best it can with its human logic to connect dots and come up with a cause-and-effect explanation. It does this in part because you are curious creatures, always wanting to understand yourselves and the world around you. This response in you is automatic, as mind and its powers are so central to who you think you are. But your mind also does this to attempt to document the cause-and-effect chain that lead to that experience so you can ensure that happy and wonderful things can be recreated again later while ensuring that unhappy and awful things can be avoided and stopped in their tracks later. Essentially, as your soul learns through your human self making choices and dealing with the consequences, your human self is learning simultaneously through the lens of 3D logic, watching what happens and assigning meaning to all the good and the bad as you go.

The problem with this is that 3D logic is very different from the logic of soul. The former is rooted in and grows from a mechanical conception of the world you see in front of you as and interpret to be reality, which you elevate to the status of truth. Your linear, logical mind is rooted in the need for proof, and it looks to the material world to provide it. The logic of soul operates according the truth that vibrations create the 3D world around you: Whatever you vibrate (think, feel, and believe) is what you will experience as the manifest world surrounding you. There is a stark disconnection between these two ways of seeing things, and it is my intentions to teach you to live according to the logic of soul so that you can be happier, saner, healthier, and more present so you can do what matters most to you. But you are deeply attached to that mind of yours and its insistence that 3D is all that's real! Take the opportunity as I describe karma in these pages to make a commitment to honestly evaluate how your mind works. Look at how you receive my words and what kind of reactions might come from your mind. Be aware that the mind often generates defensive tactics to try to protect you, but if you are drawn to read this text, you may be energetically driven to do so by a different part of you, one what wants a truth bigger than the confines and limitations of your linear, logical mind.

So, this karma business is about you as an energetic being vibrating into manifestation in front of you what you think, feel, and believe. You are a portion of All That Is, which is Divine Consciousness, and what you think, feel, and believe is Divine Law. You didn't realize that you're that powerful, did you? Well, you are. You are making everything in your life happen because on some level, whether conscious or unconscious, you expect it to happen.

Did you know that your unconscious self is also vibrating these commands? This is, in fact, the key to understanding the multilife, multidimensional issues with slavery and other intense issues. It's highly unlikely that you were born, sold, or abducted into slavery in this life. But as you read this text, you might resonate deeply with some or all of the descriptions of the hows, whys, and whos of slavery it contains. You may identify with one or more of the themes of disempowerment I'm describing as going hand-in-hand with slavery of all kinds all across the Earth timeline. Remember that every single one of you has both been owned and has owned others at different points all along the Earth timeline – no soul has opted out of this very important opportunity to learn about these particular levels of the power over/power under games available to all souls so many human lives. If you have not lived as a slave in this life, how could you identify with these themes, how you could you feel that they are part of who you are and have been? The answer is that you are now carrying and, at times, feeling the rising up to the surface of themes and feelings from your soul's multiple lives. They are stored in your unconscious, and they vibrate powerfully!

And so what is happening in your life all the time is that you are vibrating certain thoughts, feelings, and beliefs consciously while you are also vibrating certain thoughts, feelings, and beliefs unconsciously.

Each category is equally powerful, and that you sometimes get mixed results when you set positive, life-affirming intentions is due to this fact. You might consciously vibrate that other people are helpful and available, a chosen belief you may have adopted intentionally. Yet you might simultaneously unconsciously vibrate a karma from another life – a belief attached to a painful experience elsewhere on the timeline – that no one will help you. The unconscious belief will, being just as powerful as the conscious belief, confuse, fog over, or in a way cancel out your conscious positive, life-affirming belief. You'll have this great intention and perceive that 3D is not working with you. In fact, what is happening is that you are seeing manifestations of the negative, unconscious belief. You can clear it and bring that unconscious part of yourself lovingly on board with your conscious self. It takes work, and I am here to teach you to do it.

Regarding slavery, all of the awful experiences associated with it can imprint a person deeply. And then you are born to live this life on a different part of the timeline, all the time vibrating the pain, fear, and disempowerment that this other person connected to your soul felt. While you are likely not a slave in this life, you will do what you can to avoid triggering or reliving the pain, fear, and disempowerment that the other you experienced. *It is in your unconscious, and it is driving your conscious choices because you unconsciously avoid triggering your deepest pain, fear, anger, and regret as a survival mechanism.*

As one example, imagine someone kidnapped into slavery on some part of the Earth timeline. This person lived an independent life with her family and community, doing the kinds of things her people had always done including their particular culture including work, art, and religion. Upon becoming a captive, she is told that she cannot live as she did and must adopt the way of life her captors expect and demand that she live. For her, the main thing that she perceives keeps her who she's always been is her religion. In this new place, she is no longer allowed to practice the rituals her people had always practiced. Maybe there's a new religion her captors force upon her, or maybe they refuse their captives their chosen religion or any sort of religion at all. This hurts her deeply and her emotional health is starting to affect her slave work. This is noticed by the captors and perhaps, after enough of these issues, in her work, she is punished. Now, she knows that the problem is that she's losing herself because she's not allowed to pray in her own way to her gods or ancestors, but she also knows that her captors and the overseers care nothing for her happiness and emotional health. They've already made it clear that they don't care about anything but how hard and how much she's working. They banned her or all religion, after all – they've made their position clear, and they control the food, safety, and everything else every hour of every day.

As her work suffers, she is beaten or otherwise punished in whatever way the slavers deem appropriate. Maybe this happens once or twice, maybe a hundred or a thousand times. But the woman's mind will at some point develop beliefs about *why* it is happening. Her linear, logical mind will develop a schema to understand and contextualize herself, her behavior, her choices, the fact that she has been captured and enslaved, why she's being punished, who these slavers are and how they can do this to anyone, why they can do this to her, what did she do to deserve this, etc. It is potentially an endless list of possible questions and the answers to them, depending on many factors.[4] Each of you does this every single

---

[4] Different people going through the same experience can come out the other side with vastly different conceptions of

one of your human lives, and you most of the time don't even realize that you're doing it. You live through the lens of your linear, logical mind as you are taught to do, with the emphasis on logic and reason that permeates your collective idea of who you as humans are.

This incredibly difficult life unfolds as it does for as long as it does. Maybe she is set free at some point for some reason, maybe she dies in captivity from abuse, illness, or naturally from old age at some point. But the emotional and energetic imprint has taken place first with the pain of being captured, separated from home and family, not being able to practice her religion, and then with the punishment for not working as hard, much, or well as her captors expect.

I want to impress upon you that whether she is freed or dies in captivity in some way, the imprint of the pain from disconnection with her (religious) identity and the subsequent abuse for not working hard enough will last. Imagine her freed at some point, perhaps back to the loving, welcoming arms of

---

why it happened, why it happened to them, and what it meant. Each human interprets the events of his and her life in terms the unique karmic (his or her stored belief-emotion aggregate) profile his or her soul is learning through that particular human life.

34

her family and community. They may not understand why she has nightmares and can't let herself trust people. They may think it strange that she doesn't participate in community activities since her return, and that she doesn't talk to many people as she did before she left. They're so happy to have her back and want her to be happy to be back, too. In important ways she is, but the power of the emotional/energetic imprint might still be so strong that she's not open to being reconnected to them in the ways that they expect.

Then imagine that this woman's life is a life of a soul also living as a boy born in 20th-century America. He is born to a well-adjusted, relatively normal and productive family in some part of the country and with one skin color and religion or another. In his unconscious are stored the imprints of that woman's disconnection from her home and family, the banning of her freedom to pray as she desired and needed to pray, and the abuse for not working hard, long, or well enough. These unconscious imprints of hers will drive his conscious behavior because he will do all he can to avoid feeling certain things, and these will include the pains and fears of the other-life woman captured and made a slave.

His family won't understand why he seems to be unmotivated to do much of anything or socialize with people his own age. They may be confused that he doesn't want to engage with the world around him and take advantage of all they've done to make his life happy and healthy. They might wonder why he wants to spend all of his time alone, why he doesn't trust authority figures, or why he can't handle being around people who feel anger. He himself won't understand any of the sources of his behavior, such as the fact that being alone most of the time and doing little prevents others from having the opportunity to judge what you're doing and how you're doing it or be angry with you for any reason. Because he doesn't understand these unconscious sources of energy and emotion, he won't be able to articulate what's going on. He'll just live his life as best he can to avoid being triggered in a deep way that might unearth what he fears is under the surface but can't name.

At some point, an opportunity to develop or express his talents and gifts will present itself. His conception of why this is happening and what it could mean for him and his future might end up being filtered through the lens of the woman's painful life from the other part of the timeline. The boy might still feel what the woman felt in her life, and he could be somehow unconsciously resigned to the meaningless of things, as the woman was after her horrible experiences being kidnapped, enslaved, and beaten. In other words, this boy might not want to take this wonderful opportunity because this other-life self, always with him in his unconscious, has given up because of *her* terrible experiences.

Again, even if the woman had been freed at some point, she might not have recovered from being a slave and all that went with it. The boy might live a withdrawn, disconnected life centuries later because *she* did; felt she had no other choice given what had happened to her. Each day he has the opportunity to choose not to repeat her life, but the unconscious beliefs in a person can be extremely strong. And the thing is that this is not the only life that he is unconsciously reliving! You have lived many thousands and millions of lives all across the Earth timeline, with certain themes in common. What in your unconscious might drive your conscious self in any given period of time might be related to a life or two, or a dozen, as you endeavor with your conscious self to navigate around the belief-based triggers that all those people had as a result of their own personal experiences on their parts of the timeline.[5]

See how incredibly complex it is to be human? I mean, you know this from being one, but these unconscious dynamics and their power in vibrating your life into manifestation around you is quite a story. Your linear, logical minds are mostly focused on material-world pursuits, avoiding whatever energetic and emotional land mines might make themselves obvious. Your mind-based self will, at times, accept consuming media containing themes and expressions that relate to what you feel inside, but it's for those other people to experience. That most of your media is fictional gives you a chance to in tiny ways experience the observation of certain feelings and themes without your linear, logical mind having to give up the control necessary to admit unconscious pain into conscious awareness. Your mind will, in other words, let you view certain entertainments while making sure you're not inspired to remember by letting the unconscious up from under the surface. That film or novel ends, and your mind is happy that you can go back to your power over/power under

---

[5] See *The Soul's Journey III: A Case Study* for an astrological exploration of this human experience by the channel.

fears and pursuits and return to being occupied with numbers and material-world tasks.

As you learn to navigate the reality that you are multidimensional – that you are shaped by your other-life selves' experiences all across the timeline – and how to work with and release the beliefs associated with them, you connect more and more to the wisdom of your soul. Below I will explain more about owning your creation – your life as it has been and now is – but for now in this discussion of karma, please understand that you are vibrating your painful experiences from many lives into manifestation because you believe (even if unconsciously) things about why things happen.

This boy might unconsciously believe many things that inspire, lead to, and reinforce various forms of unhappiness, all of which would have been shaped by his other-life woman's experience being captured, enslaved, and beaten as she was. The following table offers a few of the myriad possibilities.

A Belief the Boy Could Unconsciously Carry	The Source in the Woman's 3D Experience
I can't do what matters to me.	Not being able to worship in her own way.
I can't do anything well enough.	Being beaten for not working hard, enough, or well.
I don't feel at home anywhere.	Being forcibly disconnected from her home and people.
I'm disconnected. I'm with people but feel alone.	
I don't know where I belong.	
No one understands me.	Living a life being forced to live on others' terms.
Nothing matters./What's the point of anything?	Pessimism or nihilism due to feeling disempowered due to all of the above.

The woman's experience will shape her attitudes in one way or another, and the boy's unconscious self will carry them. This is how it works for all of your soul's human lives, for the record, and you've had many.

What I'm here terming "karmic inheritance" is to point out to you that you are in many serious and important ways living out the vibrational residues of your soul's other lives. Your soul is having you experience certain things to learn to go from fear into love, and it is the imprints of fear from these many lives spread out across the Earth timeline that you carry and that affect you now. *The inheritance is that, as you are powerfully vibrating emotional and energetic things into existence, you are picking up where many other-life yous have left off.* Ideally, you are choosing to bring love to the fear, pain, and powerlessness that these other yous have experienced. It is my intention for you that you choose to own what you vibrate and what is thereby manifest in front of you. This will enable you to step into your power as a Divine being by choosing to love all the hurt and damaged-feeling parts of you. *You can never be broken by hardship and pain unless you choose to give up in the face of fear and pain.*

You can change karma by changing your beliefs about why things generally or in particular happen to you. The repetition of karmic scenarios looks to many of you like a kind of destiny or fate, but it is, in reality, the manifestation of what you have for so long (and in many lives) unconsciously vibrated because of the experiences of many other-life yous. Essentially, you have inherited your own multilife beliefs! That they keep happening in the material world around you may seem to mean that the difficulty is inescapable, but you can interrupt the manifestation process by changing your mind about the painful and disempowering things that have happened to you and may be happening now. You can rewrite the narrative your mind has written and attached to the facts of what happened.[6]

And so with the woman and the boy of my example, what does it mean that she experienced what she did? Her linear, logical mind could come up with all manner of disempowering ideas that are perfectly logical ... according to her linear, logical mind. And a lot of what she came up could be similar to what your mind in her situation would come up with if you were in the same position. *But it is the logic of soul, of energy manifesting into 3D to show you what you are vibrating so you can choose to go from fear into love, that is needed here.*

In adjusting to incorporating the logic of soul into how you see your life, realize that I am asking you to add a layer to how you already see things. Your mind

---

[6] See *Conscious Revolution: Tools for 2012 and Beyond* for further discussion of how other lives affect your current life and how to work consciously with this fact.

will always develop a reason for why something happened (so it can have a sense of cause-and-effect so that you can protect yourself later), and this is normal and natural. I strongly encourage you to refuse to shame yourself because your mind does this. Do not stop the mind, do not block it, do not hate or resent it. This part of you is important. But add to its input a layer of interpretation that is based in the truth that a challenging experience could only be in your life if you carry something under the surface that needs resolution, empowerment, and release.

How this works: Something challenging happens and you're frustrated or upset that it's happening. You acknowledge that you feel this way, and you pay attention to the narrative your mind is developing about why you have to go through this, why it has to be you, what stupid thing did you do to deserve this, etc. You honor the feelings and thoughts that come up. Then you take a step back and look at what purpose this challenge could possibly serve. You assume it's there for a good reason – such as so that you can move beyond something limiting or so you can learn to own and integrate a part of you that might have been disowned or dormant – and you decide to own it as an energetic creation of yours (even if unconscious) that you can use to grow and move into more health.

This is tricky because most of you identify with the expectations, requirements, demands, and complaints of your linear, logical mind. You've thus far highly likely given it power over how you see your life, others, and the world around you. What I'm suggesting is that you also bring in a bird's-eye view on it so that you can connect more with the wisdom of soul, which recognizes that life is not supposed to be about ease, happiness, and fields of pretty flowers in which you can laze indefinitely and never have to experience pain and difficulty. Remember that all souls require all manner of happy and unhappy experiences while human in order to learn about the full range of human possibility along the path to becoming the source of love for the self and inhabiting the loving wisdom of soul.

Choose to let yourself feel what you feel in response to what happens in your life. But ensure that the reactionary frustration, impatience, and criticisms of your linear, logical mind are not the final meaning attached to why something happens. Your mind does not want growth opportunities as your soul does! It wants to control everything so its goals can be met (so you can feel good about yourself for being productive, strong, and in charge of your life – powerful in some externally derived way that bypasses the wisdom of soul entirely) and its fears can be avoided (so it doesn't have to confront anything it doesn't already know and understand).

I am speaking of a deep empowerment process you can choose to undertake in order to interrupt these karmic cycles of manifestation that challenge you so. Nothing could be in your life if it didn't serve a purpose. The pattern that makes you unhappy or leaves you feeling blocked or unloved/unlovable is with you to show you that it's vibrating as a truth in your unconscious. *All beliefs can be changed, and so all karma can be changed.* The karmic inheritance of slavery is a difficult set of beliefs to undo, but it is entirely possible. Because slavery involves so much tearing apart families, kidnapping, confining, beating, raping, molesting, killing, and other violence, the imprints in your field may be extremely deep. A conversation about slavery will, in many cases, naturally lead to a conversation about healing trauma. I will discuss this later in the text, after I have finished exploring inheritance in further detail.

Ancestral Inheritance

The other kind of inheritance to be covered here is one in line with how you typically think of this term: What your family, ancestors, and community hand down to you. In very important ways, the flow of this energetic pathway (from those who come before in terms of linear time to those who come after) can serve to define who a person believes he or she is. A person could be born generations after his or her ancestors' experience with slavery, but the residues and related effects can be present in his or her energy field and consciousness (including his or her unconscious) during the entirety of life if not addressed and released.

Here I will discuss two avenues of energetic transmission, what happens to a developing fetus during the mother's pregnancy and the energetic absorbency of the child following birth. But I also want to address a third that is floating around quite a lot when talk like this comes up. Some of you have heard much about cellular or DNA-based transmission of ancestral issues, but I want you to know that that this, in fact, a misunderstanding. If a disempowering ancestral pain or anger is in your cells, it is because you as an individual being have absorbed something from your people (and this happened because your

46

souls are in cahoots in the conspiracy of love I keep mentioning here), not because it is chemically encoded in your cells.

If you conceive of these ancestral transmissions as based in DNA, your linear, logical mind will take you into a trap. It will take over with an assumption that these issues can't be addressed, changed, and released, because – after all – you can't change your DNA. But these beliefs and energetic imprints most certainly can be changed. Everything in your life and world is entirely energy and consciousness (including the unconscious), not about molecules that can't be altered. Your molecules are affected by your energy field, but this sort of thing doesn't start in your molecules. Consider how disempowering it is to confront that the brick wall of your science (which is to be considered infallible and worshipped) tells you that something is the way it is because of 3D rules. Now you are learning more about how things actually work – this vibrational model of the logic of soul – and you can begin to leave behind the black-and-white assumptions that might have been ingrained in you by your linear, logical mind choosing to rely solely on what is manifesting in 3D reality as the be all, end all truth.

During gestation, the fetal child absorbs the energies and emotions in and around the mother. Obviously, the mother is the primary influence while others come and go on a day-to-day basis, and the developing fetus is exposed to whatever it is that's going on. If the child is born via the vaginal canal, the baby is imprinted with certain ancestral memories and imprints on the way out. These are filtered through the lens of the mother's consciousness, such that if the mother has made peace with, for example, an ancestral pattern of a problem with anger, the baby will be imprinted with this history in a different way than if the mother has not made peace with such an ancestral pattern. If she is confused, resentful, defensive, or something else vibrating on the fear spectrum, the baby will receive not only the energetic data but also the mother's disposition regarding it.

Starting immediately after birth, the baby energetically begins absorbing whatever it is that surrounds him or her. All energies related to how the family deals with psychological, emotional, political, economic, religious, and all other issues can and do make an initial imprint upon the child. In a way, the baby is born into emotional and energetic weather events that have already been in the process of unfolding and that dominate and define the scene.

When negativity, powerlessness, anger, and other emotions define this early environment, no one is to blame, to be sure. The soul of the child has opted to cocreate family with these other souls experiencing and feeling these human dramas, and the agreements between souls are based in love so that they all give each other the opportunity to go from fear into love over the course of lifetimes, the point of your soul opting to be human in the first place.

Even if removed by generations or many hundreds of years, it is possible for the effects of major issues in the family history to be present in offspring in current generations. The members of the family may not be aware that this has happened and, again, no one is to be blamed when it does because it is a normal human function of family as intended and set up by all the souls involved. The soul knows its human baby selves in each of its many lives will be helpless and clueless, and it makes agreements based in love for its human selves to be conditioned by people already on the Earth plane – family. Even when the human side of things is difficult, abusive, neglectful, etc., the agreements between the souls is always based in love so each member of the family has the opportunity to learn to go from fear into love on his or her own. Examples of these energetic transmissions include famine, persecution, genocide or attempted genocide, slavery, the loss of children or grief in general, poverty, loss of faith, and being socially, politically, or economically marginalized for some reason.

When an energetic/emotional thread is handed down in a family in this way, all the souls in the system have chosen to learn about how to process this kind of thing. It is part of what we might call the "karmic homework" they as souls have agreed to attempt to work out together. Often when a person becomes aware of one of these huge issues that's not been effectively dealt with and resolved after many generations, it can seem to the person too big to deal with. He or she might feel overwhelmed by the karmic- or fated-feeling density and weight of the energies in question.

When the effects of slavery are handed down as such a karmic family energetic inheritance, there are many potential effects within that family. Not all families will be full of these unhappy situations, but if you know there is slavery in your ancestral background, be attuned to how certain energies might have defined or dominated your family system's history and make a commitment to root through your own energetic inheritance and identify any of these sorts of feelings. Anger, rage, defeat, self-righteous defensiveness, addictions, abuse, suicidal tendencies or success, loss of faith in life or God, doubts that life is supportive and people kind, fears for safety and security, marginalization, depression, anxiety, and many other things are possible to be floating around energetically in a family system. It can be a mix of these things in a given family, so that this particular relative is self-destructive because of stifled anger and aborted creativity while this other one acts out upon others abusively for whatever reason. It can also be one or two of these things that seem to repeat unfortunately in each or most generations, while different members of the family system try to figure out how to process the intense pain, fear, or anger that's been handed down through generations.

Remember the above discussion about karma and how every human is constantly vibrating into manifest reality around him or her what he or she thinks, feels, and believes. *Those with slavery in their ancestry might view the effects of the vibration in their unconscious (what is happening in front of them) as legitimately reinforcing what their families taught or modeled them to believe about life, other people, the self, possibilities, God, etc.* If this is you, realize that

51

you must interrupt what it seems to mean that you are manifesting these things in your life. If you choose to accept the big picture perspectives on slavery and soul offered in this book, you will find yourself able to recognize that slavery itself exists for reasons that have everything to do with individual and collective soul growth regarding what power is and isn't here on Earth while human. You will also be able to view what your family and ancestors experienced with a compassion that can become a detached love for the trials and tribulations that humans go through as their souls learn how to go from love into fear over the course of so many lifetimes spread out all along the Earth timeline. Finally, you will be able to work intentionally and from a grounded, sane, loving place with whatever energetic inheritances you might have taken on and need to reframe and release. You'll be able to bring a loving compassion to the histories of pain, anger, fear, and disempowerment that have dogged your family for so many generations, bringing you closer to your true nature as Divine beings, All That Is that is always loving, compassionate, and accepting.

There could be obvious patterns handed down and lived out by people in each generation, but sometimes it's carried yet not lived out. For example, if there is a pattern of destructiveness of self and/or other in your family, your immediate family members might in some way carry it but not live that way. All people with ancestors who lived through slavery must ensure that they have not internalized any of the disempowering effects even if they are not driven to recreate disempowered and disempowering behaviors that many people in that situation might. For instance, alcoholism or abuse might have been a family pattern for generations until your parents refused to treat their children that way. The effects of abuse over generations may be handed down energetically to you, and the anger, pain, despair, and anything else that originally inspired the abuse and could have been seeded by the aftermath of slavery could be in your field as well. As you consider the histories of your family, be aware of the generational hand-me-down trends that can affect those in generations long after the end of slavery.

Dehumanization

Some of you have learned that you have lived just a handful of lives on Earth, and some of you have a sense that you have not been here before. Yet the way it actually works is that you live many, many lives here on Earth sprinkled all over the timeline. You live thousands and millions of lives as humans and all kinds of animals, and some of these lives are very short relative to the human life you are presently living.

Regarding animal life, if an animal has agency, it has consciousness. And this means that a soul – a portion of All That Is or Divine Consciousness – is associated with it, is living that life. For the purposes of helping you understand the kinds of things you are to learn as a human, I frequently leave out information about your lives as animals. I don't want to confuse things by loading you up with too much information you might not be sure how to process, and I usually want you to focus on the human trip you're presently living out. But in relation to this teaching about slavery, it needs to come up.

Sometimes, being owned by a human as an animal is in some ways akin to slavery as a human, though of course not exactly the same. In many contexts as an animal being owned by a human, you don't have free will and can't make your own choices. Essentially, a human decides if, when, and how often you will eat, if you are going to live or die, and a human decides if you are useful (and if not, this can lead to a decision that you are going to die). You have no voice. You matter only if you can do something for that human and for as long as you can do it.

Look at it this way: Being an animal owned by a human is a chance for a soul to experience one kind of power dynamic, which contributes to souls learning how to go from fear into love, a main reason why souls incarnate as humans. There are animals that humans have decided do not think and do not have emotions. It is true that there are numerous "grades" of central nervous systems in various species and that these determine how sentient you consider an animal to be. For instance, you have stories of a primate who paints and has learned sign language, one who has learned to communicate with humans. This is real, and blows the minds of some people when they find out about it. They don't know where to file this information because millennia of human conditioning states with certainty that humans are the apex of evolution and that language and how amazingly clever you are set you apart from the animals. While these stories exist, you have other animals you have decided cannot possibly create or communicate in any meaningful way. For most of you most of the time, animals are resources. Often they are vehicles for doing work and/or making money, externally projected images of what power is and means. Those you keep in your home are there for support and companionship, to make you feel less alone and to bring more love and friendship into your lives. Some of them do work for you in protecting or guarding your home, too, but many are there so that you can hope to feel less alone and more loved.[7]

A main way of determining that those who are different than you and your group should be owned, controlled, and used through slavery is that you ascribe to them qualities and traits that are not human or, perhaps, you decide they are subhuman. You can get it into your heads that those other people are animals, or maybe just not quite human enough to deserve the freedom and self-directed agency as you do. You may identify your self-image as the image of God or a god, making you special while those other people are below you. One of the points I wish to make for you in this teaching is that as absurd as it is for many of you in this day and age that a person with a skin color different than yours should be thought of as not human or not as human as you are, for millennia this has been happening in individual human

---

[7] The channeled book *Approaching Love* includes a treatment of humans' relationships with animals as food and as pets, with emphasis re the latter on cats and dogs.

and group minds regarding animals as well as other people. If you are able to use cows and other animals to do your work so you can make money, why not use those other people who are not as important to God as you are to make money? It's easy for humans to decide that others who are not like you are not made in the image of God and, therefore, here to be used as resources for you. Historically, many of you have firmly believed that all other life on the Earth was put here for you by some patriarchal god to use for your benefit and so that you can do that God's "good work."

This should horrify you. It should do so for a number of reasons, not the least of which being that you have been on both sides of this dynamic all over the Earth timeline. This is not to say that you are or have been necessarily a bad person because you think this way. Instead, you should contextualize this as indicative of the fact that you, as a portion of All That Is, have been and are learning about conceptions of power and what it seems to require to get, maintain, and increase it.

It should also horrify you because at this point on the Earth timeline you are more sensitive than ever to the energies in the world around you. You are picking up at unprecedented levels the energies and therefore emotions of other people and those floating around in your environments, and you are also picking up on the energies behind activities and situations. And this increasing sensitivity will continue. This means that you are (unwittingly, most of the time) sensing the frequencies that have informed and motivated the generation of products and processes that you encounter and consume. This is a gift the souls of those living on this part of the Earth timeline have given their human selves, but it can often feel to the humans like a burden and one that you do not wish to experience. But it is part of your collective, long-term development of learning that you are energetic beings, not your names, biographies, brains, professions, aversions, preferences, shame, choices, or histories. Being conscious of being an energetic being means experiencing life in a multidimensional way, with the barriers between levels of your consciousness dissolved or dissolving. Your unfolding multidimensionality is the reason memories and fears sourced in other lives are coming to the surface as much as they are these days, leading some to wonder if they are emotionally or mentally ill or on the express train to it. What is happening, in fact, is that your fears, pains, and dilemmas from many lives are rising to the surface and coalescing in your day-to-day consciousness now. It can be confusing, and you must decide to become and stay grounded enough to be able to learn from these situations what you need to in order to resolve the fears and dilemmas and integrate those threads of your multidimensional consciousness.

You are not what has happened to you, what others have told you, or what you think about yourself or the world. You are not your hopes and fears or your desires. You are an energetic being. And now you are being challenged to learn about that on the fly, seemingly with no net, so to speak. If you feel that you have been dropped into some sort of deep end with no floaties to rely on, realize that you have. But know that it's not bad news – you are simply being asked to evolve your willingness to allow more kinds of information and realities into your consciousness to tell you more who you really are – beyond your conditioning, and beyond your (brain's) notions of who you are and what your life is about.

Multidimensionality and Power

These days, you are experiencing a variety of kinds of uncertainty, fear, and pain coming to the surface. You also should be noticing a certain sort of rawness regarding your hot-button issues, meaning that you are more sensitive and may be more reactive to what has for much of your life bothered you about your choices, others, the world, etc. What's happening is that new layers of your soul's awareness that have been embedded in your unconscious are coming into focus. Your soul's awareness tracks all of your many lives, cognizant of all of its human manifestations and their adventures and issues. What your soul's other human selves fear will come up in you now, as described in the section above on karmic inheritance. What those other selves desire will come up, too. What hurts in their lives will now inspire in you a sense of hurt.

Just to be clear, with all these old things getting louder and new things coming up, know that you are not ill. You are not crazy. If you are feeling imbalanced it is because you have not yet learned to manage all of these elements of consciousness through becoming grounded and adapting your willingness to define yourself to include the reality of multidimensionality. Since October of 2011, when the Mayan Long Count Calendar ended, the veils between dimensions have been dissolving, leaving you feeling more of your multiple lives across time but, likely, not having a context in which to understand your deepening experience. Over the following 14 months (until the Winter Solstice of 2012), processes began for you that you are now dealing with in important, time- and energy-consuming ways because you are being invited to evolve your sense of yourself as an energetic being with consciousness that exists across time and how to manage the reality of that truth.

As I said in the beginning of this text, all of you have been on both sides of the kinds of power dynamics that slavery describes and creates. The painful feelings and disempowering beliefs attached to them will come up in your emotional field in many places along the Earth timeline. You have all also in many lives had to deal with the effects of slavery on your loved ones, your descendants, your ancestors, your cultures, and your communities. This is a global issue coming to a head now because the separations within your consciousness between your souls' many lives are dissolving, due to the beginning of the maturation process marked by the end of the Mayan

Long Count Calendar. *It is not in the natural order of things to remain hurt, imbalanced, and unresolved. What needs resolution, release, and healing must and will come to the surface to be resolved, released, and healed.*

Many people all over the planet are in different ways waking up to the sense that they no longer need buy into someone else's or some institution's idea that they should be less than wonderful, self-loving, and self-determining. There are so many people now who are feeling an intense and resonant call to move into more empowered ways of being, and you cannot be empowered if you are still locked into dated conceptions of what a human is and who deserves freedom and autonomous, self-directed agency. The process of coming back into balance can be thought of as a healing process. It involves refeeling and re-experiencing painful dynamics, which is where you are now, learning to integrate the lessons, see the multidimensional truth that you have experienced something for good reason that your soul set in motion, and then moving on. On Earth at the present time, this is happening loudly regarding numerous issues including government and corporate power, how everything that is feminine has been treated by whatever is masculine, what you think of as race relations, and power over/power under games including abuse, rape, human trafficking, and slavery.

To your day-to-day awareness that tends to be based in mind and personality, it might seem that the world is going to shit. If you tune into any news source, you'll be exposed to unending listing and joy- and creativity-stunting analysis of the awful things that people are doing to each other all over the world. An epidemic of rape in South Asia, ethnic cleansing and sexual slavery in the Middle East, violent population control in East Asia, kidnapping and conscription to war in Africa, racial intolerance, tension, and violence in the United States, and others are covered over and over again in exhausting detail by your news media. It might look at first glance to be the worst time to be alive in the history of the planet, and there are certainly those of you in the human population who are eager to have your fears about the imminent end of the world proven correct so you can have some sense that you've been right all along to live with and in fear.

Yet this fear is sourced in the fact that you carry intense fears from all over the Earth timeline that are coming up in your field now, and you are at present not sure how to interact with a world that is not inspiring it. A world in which all of these things happening are seen to be healing opportunities would mess up the parts of some people who are not sure how to deal with and overcome their terror and dread concerning their fears. It is not true that the world is going to shit – you are all in a massive, unprecedented healing crisis and so your shit is coming to the surface to be addressed, understood, resolved, and released. Every single one of you is a Divine being learning to become the source of love yourself, and this healing crisis in large part centers on your struggle to leave behind fears and doubts that there is not enough (love) and that you are separated from the Divine, that you must fight others for who has the right to stand up in a sense of moral correctness about what is happening on Earth. It is painful, yes, and yet it is necessary.

For those who are tempted to lose faith because of what you see in and hear about the world, know that this is temporary and that you can choose to bring the energy you want to see in the world with you. It takes getting grounded and incorporating all the teachings I offer to you in this series of channeled books. It takes courage to stand up with love in the face of fear, pain, sorrow, anger, regret, shame, guilt, and other disempowering energies and emotions.

Powerlessness is one of the themes that goes with the experience of slavery. Another is what one has to do to deserve to be able or allowed to survive. A third is the experience of different costs to survival and how they can affect one's self-conception and willingness to be aligned with love. Yet another is the challenge of breaking through apparent realities of powerlessness in order to see the truth of what power really is and how it really works. But there are many themes that those who live through the lens of slavery are exploring as portions of All That Is.

In daily life, some of you are now feeling a sense of powerlessness in the face of corporations, governments, families, other people, and circumstance that can trigger karmic memories and feelings of other places on the Earth timeline in which your other-life selves are living as slaves. As explorations of power are necessarily central to all human journeys, many factors during these times you are living in will seem to conspire to bring up questions of just how much power you have. Again, it is not in the natural order of things that tension remain unresolved and experiences unintegrated in your emotional field, and so things must come up for review and healing. As stated above, this means re-experiencing and refeeling intense and painful emotions from many lives. This is the position that each and every one of you is in now!

You are being practically bombarded with stimulation to draw out what in your multi-dimensional/multilife energy field and consciousness is not resolved and/or still hurts and makes you feel small and powerless.

Since the end of 2011, you have been living in a time defined by the need to revisit your history and heal your relationship with and interpretation of your past. Now I hope you are clear that it is not just this life you are currently living that is being reviewed, but a great number of your soul's many lives spread out across the Earth timeline that share themes with this present-day life of yours. You are now, in your living as you with your name and your job and likes and dislikes, simultaneously reliving a number of issues from many lives. You are trying to figure out how to live, and you are dealing with all this complexity! I want you to know how to address these issues and proceed through the difficult and confusing scenarios coming to and up within you consciously, and that begins with seeing them as the growth opportunities that they are.

Consider what in your life, if anything, makes you feel powerless. If there is nothing, then you are either doing everything in tune with the Universe or you need to look deeper within and with more open eyes! This is a time in human history when all are faced with resolving the unresolved issues of the multidimensional past. How you orient yourself is everything: Is this difficult thing happening now because I deserve pain? Is this hardship somehow deserved? Am I being punished? Or is it possible that I'm being invited to resolve something that gums up my energy field and consciousness, that I couldn't possibly resolve if it were lying dormant under the surface … where it's been since I shoved it down there because it hurt too much to confront and hold in my awareness?

I guarantee you that the thing that makes you feel or perceive yourself as powerless is in your space precisely and only so that you can alter your relationship with it and, ultimately, shed the difficulty and pain you have attached to it. This is a major focus of human life on Earth now, even for those who are not what you might call spiritual or identify as being on a healing or evolutionary path. All of you are in need of revisiting the past so you can move beyond your limiting and limited conceptions of what life is, who you are, who god is, and the like.

Owning Your Creation

You as individuals and as a collective are ready to learn to see the power of your creation, and it is true that all that you have experienced reflects what you are cocreating with others and with the world around you. As portions of Divine Consciousness and All That Is, your consciousness cannot help but broadcast creative signals to the world around you, which begins to organize itself around the Divine commands that those signals issue. You are Creator Consciousness! All you have undergone has been your cocreation so that All That Is in general – and the portion of it that is your soul in particular – can learn about the wide variety of human experiences that can make up a life.

Are you willing to own all that has happened to you as your cocreation? This is not easy, but it is the path of your evolutionary growth during this portion of human history. You are in a long-term process to begin to take ownership of your creative power. The first step is, however, not so noble as that previous sentence may sound. It is in refeeling the pain from the past and altering what you think it means that it happened. When you own what you have created, you can see more about how power works when you are intentional versus not intentional, conscious of what's going on vs. unaware, when you align yourself with your truth versus don't align with it, and when you choose from fear versus faith. If you are going to travel this evolutionary road and hang out with me and other beings like me – helpers who are available to assist in your evolution no matter what you need – then you must become comfortable seeing all aspects, themes, and details of your life past and present as indicative of a long term, multilife process of learning to go from fear into love. This is the mission of all portions of All That Is – all souls – and each and every human life presents myriad opportunities to upgrade how you choose what you choose. In many ways, it doesn't matter what you choose as long you choose from a place of alignment with what is true and right for you.

All that's hurt you, all that's disempowered you, all that's made you feel small and lead to some part of you begin to wither and become sad and deflated – all of this has served your soul's journey as a human to learn about what's possible living as a human on Earth.

Dehumanization Revisited

Above I gave you an overview of the similarities of how the human collective over time has tended to treat animals and the dehumanization inherent in slavery. I now return to this topic to say more.

If humans see themselves as the apex of evolution on the planet, it is easy and simple to treat animals in abusive, violent ways, and not such a stretch to treat other humans viewed as animals in the same ways. Not all of you in a given time do this, of course, but it's a human thing that's arisen as a result of elevating yourselves above other species because of the admitted logical power of the human mind that your minds have decided to seduce you into believing is who you truly are.

Earlier I mentioned that there are different levels of central nervous systems that belong to different species. You have learned over time of the physical and biochemical differences that exist between various kinds of animals on Earth. You must realize that you are animals if you are going to make headway on healing slavery, but it is true that the human central nervous system sets you apart. It is part of the game of living on Earth, and the choice of each soul to incarnate in a given life as a member of one species or another is specific. There is no randomness and there are no accidents when it comes to what kind of physical being a soul finds itself living as in a particular life – none at all. This is fitting with the fact that different species offer souls various potential experiences when it comes to living out the themes the souls choose. Living as an animal that can do this thing but cannot do that other thing covers the need of a soul to experience life on Earth through various lenses of possibility, learning about living on the planet given different sets of variables. Regarding animals' relationships with humans, there are numerous kinds of roles that species represent. Domesticated animals as pets have particular functions, as do animals that work and provide food for humans.[8]

Identifying as the apex of evolution, humans can find themselves desiring to control as many aspects of their lives and environments as possible. All That Is sets out to learn about the infinite possibilities available to humans and other animals, and so this should not surprise any of us. Control is one kind of

---

[8] See the channeled book *Approaching Love*.

way of being to explore and so, of course, humans have pursued it. Elsewhere I have explored at length what inspired and triggered this course of control-based philosophy and behavior.[9] For now, I will say that the human collective needed to break away from its mother, the Earth as a goddess/mother figure, in order to explore what it means, costs, and results in to attempt to live through the lens of control of self, other, and the world around them. It was a necessary part of the learning journey of All That Is, and humans now are in the position of needing to heal all the things that came out of that way of living. You are easing out of patriarchal ways of being now, and many of you are working earnestly and around the clock to unwind and detach from the effects of that particular imbalanced way of living and doing.

And so, if you can control the world around you, you will play with doing so. Well, all who are different than you are part of that world! You wonder over time how it is that you might do and have all that you want, and the presence of other people can, of course, get in the way. Those other people are often fundamentally different from you in some way(s), and the difference can inspire in you a sense of pride about

[9] See the channeled book *Goddess Past, Present, and Future*.

who you are and a sense of fear or hatred (based in fear) about who they are. Your self-esteem can be challenged by the existence of others who are different than you. If you are made in the image of God (*your* god), then who are these other people with different skin color, customs, and/or religious beliefs? Well, clearly, they are not made in the image of God (*your* god), so they must be in some way bad. Or, at least, not as deserving of freedom and self-directed agency as you are.

Language is the development in the human species that has led to the superiority complex that you have developed in relation to the rest of the animals on the planet. And yet it has also proven to be a marker of difference that goes a long way toward inspiring many to fail to find common ground with the other. After all, you can't understand what they're saying! And even when you do, you may be wont to interpret differences in thought patterns and mental processing – and even classes of words in that other language the rationale for which makes no sense to you – as limits to the intelligence of the other. It is not true that different racial groups have different levels of intelligence. Intelligence in an individual is high, moderate, or low depending on many factors that have to do with the soul's choice and often does include genetics, but there are no rules and consistencies when it comes to race and intelligence. Also, there are different forms of intelligence, as you have been exploring with regard to emotional intelligence (EQ) the last few decades on Earth as separate from IQ, your standard benchmark for evaluating and ranking human intelligence.

Have you seen viral videos online of dogs seeming to say or sing "I love you"? It might catch your ear, it might open your heart, or it might make you laugh. What you are seeing now is that some animals are trying to let you know that they are able to communicate. Beyond what is known as animal communication, which has thus far been reserved for psychic or intuitive people most of you believe you could never turn out to be, animals are reaching out to you now. As part of All That Is functioning to serve humans in your evolution, animals now are trying to reach out to and connect with you in the only ways that you(r linear, logical minds) find important. Now, it's true that many of you value the emotional connection you can and do have with animals, but this a collective move toward breaking down what humans as a group tend to think animals are here for. You are in the process of waking up to the fact that they are an integral part of the fabric of life on Earth, and that they have souls. They do and are going to continue to work on communicating with you – breaking down barriers – to show you that they are in this Earth trip with you and that they are not here to be used as a resource for you and your mind's progress-oriented, concrete-pouring, money-making plans. As loving servants to All That Is just like all souls, they have a message for you: *You're an animal, too, and we're in this together. We're here for you. We can teach you more about your true nature as energetic beings with consciousness temporarily living physical lives.*

Through singing and speaking to you, they are demonstrating that they can, in fact, be connected with you through conscious communication. They are holding space for you to see that the logic of mind – and the central nervous system that comes with being a human – is not the be-all, end-all solution to everything. They are serving you by attempting to wake you up to the reality that mind, brain, and logic are not all there is. The big picture of this story is that you need to realize and own that your emotions and your energetic/emotional sensitivity matter, and you need to learn that they are integral parts of your human self. Humanity has evolved a perceptive filter regarding the importance of the power of mind

75

above all else and it is doing itself harm by living through that lens above all others. You are no longer serving yourselves by investing above all else in your cleverness and smarts.

All this said, understand that how you have treated the other as animals and other people as slaves is ready to be resolved and released. It is not, in the end, much different between other animals and people just about all cultures have dehumanized over the course of time on Earth so as to make it okay to enslave them. Dogs on viral videos doing all they can to say or sing "I love you" mark an evolutionary juncture which is to tell you that you are ready to dig into the cache of emotional memories, struggle, and pain surrounding the reality of slavery on your planet. If, in other words, a dog can tell you that he or she loves you, all of your preconceived mental constructs about the other – including what they are here for, who they are, and what you can do to them because they're not like your self-image based in your idea of who God is – are immediately out the window.

In one way, it might seem like a lot to handle. It's not just a need to resolve and release histories of slavery and the effects on families and cultures, but a need to heal a global imbalance of conception of and relationship with the other. Fear-based tribal consciousness that has you concerned about and fearing what the other might do to and about you is your enemy now, not that person with that other skin color or those weird-to-you religious beliefs and customs. You are all in this together, and getting this deeply and owning it will serve you in healing a history of slavery that's as old as humanity itself.

Perspectives

Slavers

Making the other into an image of something other than one with God (*your god*), there's no apparent problem with using the other for your own purposes. This is a fundamental to the impulse that leads a person or group of people to enslave another person or group. And if your perceived purpose is to chase external projections of power (money, influence, possessions, status, etc.), then you will enslave others and put them to work for the betterment of your economic position and that of your family and tribal group. You will care about the enslaved only insofar as they function to provide a profit in the ways you've designed to further your externally-projected power-building goals. If things are going very well economically, you may not care about the health of your slaves too much because you are more able to afford to replace them than in other times. If things are not going so well economically, then you might care more about protecting your investment, but this does not mean that you will treat those you own well. You may have no interest in their emotional, psychological, or spiritual health, and you may not care about what makes them unique individuals. If you are smart in protecting your investment, you will keep an eye on their physical health, which is likely all that you care about. They are, after all, beasts of burden. You own them. They're animals doing work.

You will perceive that you can treat your slaves in any way that you want, including sexually. They are not fully human, you have decided, and therefore don't have the same rights to say "yes" and "no" when they wish as do those fully human, and you might even see them as less than human enough to do what you please to them whenever you wish. And while they're less than human, they might still be extremely attractive to you. You can take out your anger, frustration, resentment, self-hatred for being someone who owns other people, and other emotions on them, and they have to take it. You can treat them as you would animals, and they can't do anything about it.

Yet here's what's happening outside the human, Earth-based dynamics: *Your soul has made love-based agreements with the souls of the humans you own. Their portions of Divine Consciousness or All That Is are giving you the opportunity to do what you will to them so you both learn about 3D assumptions*

79

about what power is and how to hold onto and in-crease it. They do this so that your soul has the experience while being human of conceiving of power in these externally-projected ways and acting them out; pursuing power plays and games so that you can see what it's like, costs, and means. Their souls live human life through the lens of being owned and controlled by you to give you the opportunity to experience an externally-projected definition of power: power-over. Such a definition of strength is central to All That Is cycling through human life on this planet, and it is necessary. All souls are incarnating again and again on Earth (whether as human or other animal) in order to learn to go through fear and, in the end, choose love.

No souls can be damaged by human experience, no matter what happens to or is done by a human. The damage that occurs is stored as rents, dents, and scratches in and on a person's emotional body. *The soul is never wounded.* Karma between people is real, consisting of the perception of energetic credit and debt between them. No matter what a person does, the soul is not damaged, but an accounting will happen between that person and others upon whom he or she acts in various capacities. And so when these dynamics play out between people, there is from the souls' points of view a Divine service that is playing itself out. Each soul gives the others the chance to explore these power dynamics while living as humans. The souls thank each other for the opportunity, and much that the soul incarnated in the first place to experience and learn through is experienced and learned through.

Slaves

When you are a slave, you are kidnapped, stolen, bought, sold, and/or captured. You are treated as an animal. You are shown clearly what will happen to you if you do not do what is expected and required of you. You have no free will, and you have no voice. You have no say in how your body is used in any context, no matter what you are feeling, thinking, or experiencing. You are a tool for the profit and, perhaps, pleasure of another, and nothing else about you matters. No matter who you are or what you can do, you are replaceable and therefore expendable.

You may lose your name, often your family and ancestry connection, perhaps your language. You usually lose your religion and way of praying, your music, culture, and art. You are taken from home and the place you are forced to work and live in is never truly your home. It can become your home only if you give up all sense of who you are, have been, and could be.

Violence and the threat of it are used to control you. Your daily life is full of the threat or reality of beating, starvation, burning, whipping, and all other manner of brutality if you do not do what you are supposed to do. And even when you do what you are supposed to do, you may still be treated violently periodically – if not more often – just to keep you aware of who is in charge. In the end, you learn that sometimes even when you do something right, you're not doing it right, and you are punished.

The person or people who own you have absolute control over your destiny. Over time, you lose your ability to have a sense of self outside the violence done to you and your reaction to it. This happens either through atrophy and learned helplessness, or through repeated violence that cuts you off from a sense of being a person. You develop one, more than one, or all of the following intense emotions that affect you, your loved ones, and your health: anger, rage, depression, anxiety, trauma/shell shock, bitterness, apathy, hatred of self and other, a sense of nihilism, meaninglessness, pessimism, the will to do violence to self and other, an unwillingness to trust, a lack of ability to relax and enjoy life. You feel hated, and you hate. You take on violence and don't know how to release the energy in healthy ways, leading to self-harm, stuffing the energy/becoming a time bomb, and/or harm to others.

Yet from the souls' point of view, this is what's happening: *Your soul has made love-based agreements with the souls of the humans who own you. Their portions of Divine Consciousness or All That Is are giving your soul the opportunity to be acted upon through one kind of power dynamic that's about control and use of others.* They do this so that your soul has the experience while being human of conceiving of power in these externally-projected ways and having them acted out with and upon you; pursuing power plays and games so that you can see what it's like, costs, and means. Their souls live human life through the lens of owning and controlling you to give you the opportunity to experience an externally projected definition of power: power-under. Such a definition of strength is central to All That Is cycling through human life on this planet, and it is necessary. All souls are incarnating again and again on Earth (whether as human or other animal) in order to learn to go through fear and, in the end, choose love.

No souls can be damaged by human experience, no matter what happens to or is done by a human. The damage that occurs is stored as rents, dents, and scratches in and on a person's emotional body. *The soul is never wounded.* Karma between people is real, and consists of the perception of energetic credit and debt. No matter what a person does, the soul is not damaged, but an accounting will happen between that person and others upon whom he acts in various capacities. And so when these dynamics play out between people there is from the souls' points of view a Divine service that is playing itself out. Each soul gives the others the chance to explore these power dynamics while living as humans. The souls thank each other for the opportunity, and much that the soul incarnated in the first place to experience and learn through is experienced and learned through.

Victimization

The human experiences of slavers and slaves are vastly different, but the explanations for what is going on behind the scenes with each are almost identical. Note that the "here's what's happening" explanations above for each of the experiences for slavers and slaves are just about the same. This is intentional, and in this section I will address some of what happens in your linear, logical mind that may make this in certain ways incomprehensible or seem unacceptable.

The totality of human experience over many lives revolves around cycling through modes of seeking to gain, develop, maintain, and grow power. All of you work through external, manifest definitions of power before you get to the truth of it, which is about an internal stance of uncompromising self-knowledge and total and absolute self-acceptance as described above.

Most humans want (or crave) power,[10] and the prevailing definitions of what it is can, of course, vary. It's safe to say, however, that all human conceptions of externally-derived and –directed power are focused on ensuring the right to express desire and free will, being safe and not subject to harm, and being secure by having resources so there is no threat of hardship, struggle, or lack. These kinds of things are the goals of this sort of search for power when it

---

[10] At minimum, the power to get, have, and maintain strength and resources to survive.

is defined by external markers. This search for external power has, for the record, been in play for as long as there have been humans living on this planet. Since you have coalesced into larger and larger communities due to the agricultural revolution, your ability to feed yourselves has strengthened but the normal animal fears of safety and survival have not changed in any way. And so as you conceive of yourselves more and more civilized as your cities and nation states gain industrial and economic power, the basic animal fears that all humans have lived with are still there, guiding things from under the surface without your knowledge. You're definitely still animals. It's just that your perception of who you are because of your building and earning power have changed.

The totality of the learning journey of souls while human centers on the need to learn to redefine power. You as a collective are at the point in your evolution as your human selves to begin to see en masse that externally-projected power is not true power. Many of you seek to know the truth about who you are and what you are doing here, and when you work with me you are perpetually invited to see beyond the meaning you have assigned to your life history and major events (and the accompanying

86

feelings, fears, and beliefs) in order to rewrite why things have happened to you. This is a process of going through what hurts and confuses you, and what you regret and hate, in order to move through the pain and into seeing the situations and others that caused it as Divine players answering the calls of your soul to help you experience all manner of human situations and the feelings, thoughts, and beliefs that result.

You cannot experience anything of import without vibrating it to you. This means that in your energy field are markers of or book marks to certain frequencies. They reflect what your soul – Goddess/God or All That Is – has decided you will experience and be changed as a result of experiencing. They also reflect your feelings and beliefs attached to feelings – karma – that you carry from past experience in this life and what has happened within and to you over the course of many lives all along the Earth timeline. When you are willing to own this, you can step into your power as a Divine being living a human life. At that point, no one is to blame for anything, not even you. There is no injustice that needs to be addressed because everything is unfolding in the ways that it needs to. In this way of being, you are able to accept with grace – a form of loving acceptance – that what has come to you in life serves your Divine purpose. And during this phase of advanced spiritual development, you can accept gently that life is not supposed to be about peace and safety alone, but about transforming the self through fear into love into a state of true, loving power. Every single one of you can get there if you are willing. Decide today that you are willing to open to that view on your life and you will, with grace, begin to step toward inhabiting the wisdom of your soul – Goddess/God or All That Is – in your day-to-day life and you will begin the process of getting there.

And so, it is true that all that you hate, refuse, reject, avoid, resent, and fear holds the key to your spiritual transformation. Facing, owning, and altering your relationship with them will take you from a disempowered human into a conscious portion of All That Is living out a human experiment on Earth, which is what each and every human life is. When you know your deepest feelings – especially the ones you fear and revile – and accept them, then you develop true power. This is the power of a conscious being seeing the multidimensional truths in play in his or her life. This sort of power is the kind that doesn't waver, that no one can take away from you, that never inspires guilt or shame, and that you need prove to no one under any circumstances. The process to get here – facing your fears and other negative, typically hated emotions and motivations – stimulates an opening within your energy field and consciousness that enlarges and reorients the lens through which you see what's happening around you. When you see the purpose of the ups and downs of your life from the vantage point of All That Is, you see that you are in charge regarding how you meet the challenges that do and will come to you. You can accept that things are on their way to greet, invite, and confront you to go from fear into love, and you are willing to see the purpose of it. This aligns your personality with the Divine wisdom of your soul, and it is the goal of All That Is in its quadrillions upon quadrillions of lives lived on the Earth as humans and animals of all kinds.

And so, you are always vibrating signals that certain kinds of things must come to you (your vibration is Divine Command, after all), and all you experience is what comes to you in response. *You are not a victim – you never have been anything of the kind.* This reorientation can be challenging for humans because it represents utter and total destruction of a worldview you have been attached to for millennia, even if recently you have begun struggling against its disempowering ethos and effects. But, friends, that worldview has kept you in and perpetuating suffering for so many of your lives! You are disempowered precisely *because of* that worldview. That frame of reference worked to a large degree for the logic of your logical, linear minds as long as you clung to manufactured images of who various gods are and what they want, expect, and demand from you. That framework functioned seemingly okay when you conceived of yourselves as clever minds with pesky bodies and annoying, overwhelming emotions that you needed to stuff deep down and avoid if you are to stay sane and productive, making enough money and gathering enough things first to survive and then to earn the respect of your peers. As you learn to open to and embrace that truth of your spiritual, energetic, multidimensional nature – that you are energetic beings with consciousnesses existing across time and living many kinds of animal and human lives on Earth all at once – the new model that asserts that you are never a victim, no matter what happens to you, makes more sense. Accepting this model of life on Earth is where all of humanity is headed.

To be fair, I want you to fully take in what it will mean for you to go through this process. You will encounter many threads of conscious selves – many

90

parts of you – that are not at first willing to give up their identities formed as a result of what has happened to (the victim who is) you. It will be a struggle at times to dig deep to find the courage to be compassionate with all of these naysayers and malcontents within you. There may be some sleepless nights and distracted or lost days as you counter the assertions of your linear, logical mind that you mustn't change nor try anything new; sort through the piles of memory-based evidence it presents as reasons you should not change in the directions I describe here. But I guarantee you that your evolution as a conscious being requires doing this, and I also guarantee that it's worth it to go through the process.

All humans must eventually overcome the apparent power of the rational mind by developing power from a choice to love unconditionally and without reservation, demoting the mind to serve the rest of their beings. As your mind judges, it approves of (loves) you and others conditionally. True power lies in loving all sides, parts, and elements of self no matter what, and your mind does what it can to fail to hear this as it refuses logics other than its own. I am asking you – no, I am charging you – to evolve beyond the limiting and limited conceptions of mind that you have developed in order to protect you. You do not need protection. You never did. If something fear-inspiring comes to you now, you are ready to see it as a reflection of fear you carry from the past and get on already with loving that part of yourself or your experience related to it, the part that vibrated that thing to you in the first place. You no longer need to perceive that you are in some way not safe – you are, after all, All That Is. You are Goddess and God. You are vibrating your world into existence all the time. You cannot help but do so – you are the Divine incarnate and what you vibrate is Divine Command and must and does become manifest.

The old model of human identity that leads to victimhood is that people and groups do things to you and you have no choice in the matter. It says that you are acted upon, and often without your consent. As a response, you have to run, hide, defend yourself, fight back, or seek vengeance (including using legal means). This way of thinking leads to self-hatred and resentment of others, and all of this kind of feeling manifests as injury and illness as it explodes out of you as various kinds of disapproval of and violence toward self and other. The mind's model of things holds that you are being acted upon and are not in charge of your reality unless you have money, power, and influence.

Tracing it back really far, it's about the perception that you are separate from Divine Source. Then you make up these rituals and religions as attempts to explain why some god is unhappy with you; create and reinforce mythologies about what you did wrong to deserve the illness, pain, injury and death that doesn't go away no matter what you do. All of you need to root out this garbage from of your consciousness immediately! Dig it up and cut it out! You've made up so many stories – and gathered them together as mythologies you call religions and then take them very seriously, even warring over whose collection of mythological stories is most true – to explain why you're not safe and instruct each other about what must be done to get the love of some god so he or she will stop punishing you. Really? People, you're clever and you can certainly spin yarns, but at this stage in the game of the evolution of human consciousness, more and more of you can agree with me that this is ridiculous.[11] I hope you're able to laugh at

---

[11] I've skipped a great deal of the explanation of victimhood your religions reflect because religions are, in fact, not the source. It's my aim here to explain to you this experience of the human perception of separateness that has driven you to conceive of yourselves as victims for one reason or another.

yourselves for endeavoring to explain the reality of injury and pain through religious mythologies. Of course you must attempt to come up with an explanation of why bad things happen. No one can blame you for that. But it has played itself out in grand style, and you are ready to finally grasp and own that all that happens to you is vibrated into existence and magnetized to you based on what you are vibrating.

How can you change this and step into being grounded in how all of this really works? First, decide that you are going to view all that exists in your life as meaningful, as a reflection of what you are vibrating either consciously or unconsciously. This will take some effort, not to mention a willingness to be humbled by realizing the truth behind some things in your life that you do not like and would not usually want to own as your creation.

Second, you must go through your life history and rewrite the narratives attached to all that has happened to you. If it was good, it was not a reward for being a good sort of person. If it was bad, it was not a punishment for being a bad sort of person. All that has happened to you has served your learning process as a soul living a human life on Earth in need of seeing your passions and fears manifest in the world around you. All that has gone down in your life that has been painful and unjust serves to teach your soul – a wonderful, loving portion of All That Is that's decided to learn about all possible human experiences – how to live on Earth and go from fear into love.

Third, make a serious and earnest commitment to yourself to own all that comes to you in the near term and far off future as a manifestation to show you what you are vibrating and own whatever that is. If you draw something that makes you afraid, for example, own that you carry fear and address it. If you draw to yourself betrayal, own that part of you hurts when betrayed. Look at all the people involved as playing a role in your soul's Divine learning journey.

Do all these things, and you will align with your soul's purpose and wisdom and your life will be so much better, happier, and less stressful. You will no longer swerve toward victimhood when you encounter something that your soul needs you to encounter so you can learn to become empowered – unflinchingly self-knowing and self-loving – by transforming relationships with various kinds of fears.

I now wish to address a category of people to whom this channeling is in large part directed. Very few, if any, who are or have been slaves in this life will encounter this material. Those who live the experience of being slaves when not slaves – those who carry the emotional signatures and fears related to this way of living – is the group in question. These people carry a karmic/multilife or ancestral inheritance of slavery that leaves them feeling that they have no free will and are going to be punished for whatever they might do. They might perceive a need to wait to be told what to do, feeling controlled, manipulated, and abused. This group of people may not experience these things from external sources but find it in the world around them as manifestations of what is carried in their energetic and emotional fields. In other words, they find it in some ways to be true even though it's not an external truth. It is happening because they fear and expect it to happen, even if unconsciously.

This is, in essence, a discussion about the imprints upon later generations and in your soul's other lives, what you commonly refer to as past lives.[12] As

---

[12] "The soul's other lives" or "your other lives" is accurate while "past lives" is not according to the soul's experience. From the soul's point of view, all of its lives are happening simultaneously. The soul exists outside time, observing its human lives unfold simultaneously all across the Earth timeline.

I have stated above in the section called "Four Truths," if you're going to make progress with healing the impacts of slavery, you must accept that all of you have experienced it in different forms and for different reasons in various parts of the Earth timeline; none of you have escaped being owned or owning others. I have also stated that not all of you carry the imprint of it in your daily lives. Again, this is because only some of you are in a position or ready to process the effects and results of slavery in any given life. As I ask you now to step up to own your life as a creation of your Divine self vibrating a world around you into existence, if you are in a life in which you need to process a history of slavery, you will come up against your fears and resistances, making evident and obvious the ways in which you feel a victim.

Know that some of you may tend to interpret a great number of benign and neutral situations and events in your life in terms of the powerlessness and fears and wounds related to it from slavery in other lives. The imprints of abuse, a loss of free will, being bought and sold as cattle, having every detail of your life interfered with by a person who owns you, and other things are what you have to resolve and release now. You have to own all that's happened to you as a creation of your soul so that it – Divine Intelligence,

All That Is – can learn about this most important pos-sibility of human life.

Disconnection

Of numerous major themes related to lifetimes of slavery, an important one is disconnection. Slavery-related varieties of it include being disconnected from a homeland (in the case of people taken from home and moved elsewhere to be slaves), family and ancestry, religion, language, community, and a sense of place in general. These and more issues relate to the root chakra in the human energy field. When this energy center is healthy, a person has and can de-velop a sense of place, a sense of community, and a connection to life and the world around him or her. When this center is imbalanced, a person can feel rootless and nomadic in a less than healthy way, as well as unsure where he or she fits within commu-nity and the world in general. The root chakra is a human's energetic foundation. Memories from other lifetimes of slavery can interfere with a person's abil-ity to feel safe and secure in a community or the world, leading to a sense of uneasiness and, perhaps discord. A person with memories from other lives of slavery coming to the surface in this life may expect and interpret criticism, judgment, and even animosity from others when there is no such intent from them. A sense of belonging in the world and having a place to be is what creates an internal foundation of safety and security, and I recommend that a person in need of these things work on the internal situation so that an outer situation reflecting a healthy root chakra can be manifested.

All souls involved in slavery across the Earth timeline are learning through the power over/power under dynamics that teach them to give up externally-projected notions of power and embrace a true, spiritual power. Being torn away from home, loved ones, and roots serves this purpose. A person is thrust into a new environment, presenting an opportunity to evaluate what he or thinks is safety, security, and support. The person may feel sadness, despair, fear, anger, and a host of other intense emotions. The person may even feel punished by life or God in addition to feeling punished by the people who have taken him or her away. But the soul envisions this as one kind of opportunity to learn to see beyond the limiting assumptions all humans carry about the nature of safety and security, and how perceptions of them tend to define who a person thinks he or she is.

Another aspect of soul-level intentions with this disconnection is to serve the need for all people to learn about each other. Transporting people from where they feel they belong and are safe begins a process of unavoidable cultural cross-pollination. The individual feels painfully uprooted while the soul is observing the person confront the opportunity to learn about the self through the lens of others from different places and with different beliefs and ways of identifying themselves. In other words, one function of slavery from the soul's perspective is to collide different cultures so that people who might have been otherwise relatively sheltered (living with their people where they were born and grew up) encounter new cultures they would not through normal processes of their homelands or villages.

Remember that the soul, a portion of All That Is or Goddess/God consciousness, comes to Earth to have all manner of experiences. I'm inviting you to look beyond the pain, anger, depression, and other heavy and intense emotions about slavery that may rise up within you as you consider the topic while you also choose to see the soul's intentions. You will heal nothing that needs healing without adding a Divine perspective to your human perspective. I ask you to commit to never denying or downplaying your feelings but to also add a layer of interpretation based in the logic of soul. In this case, that logic says that some individuals and groups need to be exposed to others' cultures in order for those souls to learn about what life is like on Earth. As all this happens through the exploitative and often abusive lens of stealing, kidnapping, using, raping, and beating each other, it may be extremely difficult for you at first to open to this.

In your time now, for most of you there are areas of your own country in which you can encounter the other. People of different skin colors and religions and those speaking languages other than your own are not that hard to find in many places in your modern world. But from the perspective of All That Is, there had to be an injection of very different people in certain places to get that started. Souls require that humans face growth opportunities, and dramatically mixing things up by transplanting individuals or large groups of people can serve this.

Another angle on the souls' intentions for this disconnection is to seed certain energies in one part of the area or globe that would not otherwise be there. I will explore this here a bit, but not in terms of an individual or two being captured or sold and enslaved near home. I will do so in the context of massed forced migrations such as the colonial slave trade that brought so many Africans from that continent to the Americas and the Caribbean, and to some of the colonizing countries in Europe.

All That Is knows that for its growth as a collective, humans need to experience discomfiting things of all kinds. The collision of cultures in all its forms brings the opportunity not just for individuals to encounter others who are different but also for cultural groups to move and anchor a different style of being in new places. Even when the culture of the transplanted people undergoes a process of attempted elimination, they carry wisdom of the cultures from their part of the Earth. Souls are souls and people are people, but this cultural cross-pollination brings in new flavors of how to be human to new parts of the globe. This is the same evolutionary opportunity All That Is required and created when Europeans found what they termed the New World and colonized it. You are reeling from the human-level damage incurred through that process, but there is a higher-level truth and need of All That Is to evolve behind every major happening on Earth. How those in the West experience the legacy of African slavery in the Americas and the Caribbean today is a story within the greater story of colonialization, which serves the collective or All That Is by introducing new cultures to new places, so all can have the opportunities to evolve through a cross-pollination that brings all into greater states of conscious awareness about what it means, costs, and requires to be human. All That Is in the form of all the humans on the globe cannot evolve in isolation! As challenging as it can be, the collision of cultures through various means is necessary for the growth of the collective.

The channel has remarked to me during this section that my explanations of these truths kind of, sort of, seem to be trying to paint this destructive history in a noble light. He has, in fact, found it a bit difficult to maintain his connection to this data stream for the last several paragraphs because part of him feels anticipatorily nervous about a perception of sugar coating these intensely painful and horrible histories. I remind him and you that you have such strong emotional reactions to the legacy of slavery (and colonization) that you have thus far not been able to see clearly any other perspective beyond victim/perpetrator dynamics. You as a collective are in a most unprecedented healing crisis centering on dredging up the painful, buried past you haven't yet figure out what to do with. You have feared the intensity of the pain and have, in effect, created a self-defeating process by which you have surrendered your power to that pain. You have given your fear all of your spiritual power because you believe pain and anger will overtake you. They exist within you, dominating the landscape. You're fooled by your linear, logical mind to believe that they are too big and awful to do anything meaningful with or about.

A major facet of the healing crisis in the collective now is to transform your relationship with your body and the Earth. What is referred to as grounding is the practice required to do this, and so you must get out of your head and into your body. And when you do, you will find a storehouse of feelings from this and other lives with which you at first have no clue how to deal. If you are familiar with my teachings, you have heard this numerous times. You will not find from me some placations and platitudes telling you that you are not alone and that all of us disembodied beings are rooting for you, as fills so much channeled material that you encounter – no. My offerings to you are invitations to evolve and to step into an empowered state as the Divine living on Earth, but you must take me up on them to derive any benefit. *Getting into your body and learning to better work with emotions from the recent and distant past is the key to the evolutionary arc you as a collective are now traveling.*

If you have had a similar reaction as the channel to this section, sit down with yourself and decide that you are stronger than pain and fear that you might carry or feel. You absolutely must cultivate a deeply grounded stance for yourself so that you can handle the reactions you might have to reading a book about how slavery and its aftermath and painful legacy serve the Divine in perfect ways! Your consciousness should be thought of as taking up space, and your body as its container as long as you live. Working to ground as a daily practice for years so to be comfortable in your body means that you are strengthening and enlarging the container, which leads to being able to handle your emotions. So, the very first step if you do not know how to deal with some feelings from the present or past is to get grounded and cultivate that practice daily and with a commitment to the long-term.

Identity

Back to our story of disconnection: If you are uprooted and feel disconnected from your sense of place, belonging, and security, then your soul has you learning something about the truth of who you really are. If you are disconnected from your ancestors, who are you? If you are removed from your home and homeland against your will, who are you? If you are dragged by force to a new country and/or continent and find yourself surrounded by others using and abusing you, who are you? What does it mean about who you are if are not where you started?

What your soul in these cases has set you on a path to learn is about what you do, can, and should use to define who you are. Mass forced migrations that lead to mass senses of disconnection such as slavery teach the souls involved what it means to lose who you think you as humans are. As Divine beings, the soul intends that you set out to figure out who you are outside the context into which you were born and in which you grew up.

The essence of what you are all now dealing with regarding the legacy of slavery is that you have defined yourselves after this disconnection in terms of the powerlessness you felt when you were taken and forced into labor.

The souls' intentions regarding slavery include what is explained above about cross-cultural pollination, seeding certain ways of being in new places on the globe, and the huge, destructive-but-Divine exploration about power over/power under dynamics at the core of slavery of all kinds. The soul never sentences you to pain but accepts that it is a natural part of the empowerment process each of you-as-humans is living so your soul (part of All That Is) can learn what it is to be human. Again, your soul is not delusional and thinking that life should be about safety and security – that delusion belongs to the parts of you yet to grow into your spiritual maturity, hoping and praying that some all-powerful and trustworthy father-figure deity will save you from each other and yourselves. But no one will save you. No one can. You are a portion of Goddess/God creating your way, having all the wonderful and awful experiences that teach it/your soul about how to live a human life.

Your soul does not view you as powerless, no matter what you experience. It is the essence of Divine Consciousness, which is loving. It sends you to the Earth plane so it can learn what it's like to be here. That you define yourself in terms of your personal and collective histories and biographies is a side-effect of you feeling disconnected from your inner divinity, which is part of the human Earth game as you learn to reconnect with your soul's loving, Divine nature. If you have a sense of the Divine within you, you don't choose to believe that you are the sum of what has happened to you or what you've chosen. When in that grounded, loving, innerconnectivity, you no longer need to hold grudges against others for what has hurt you because you accept that you are the Divine and all that has happened to and around you has been cocreated by souls in the conspiracy of love to learn about how to be human. If you adopt an identity of powerlessness, then your soul watches that unfold the same as if you adopt one of being powerful. To your soul, it's all the same – whatever you believe, however you define yourself, and however you choose to live your life.

And so as I invite you to heal many lifetimes and eras defined by slavery, I am really inviting you to redefine who you believe you are and who believe you have been. Spiritual growth requires digging through the depths of your feelings, attitudes, beliefs, ideas, and assumptions in order to move beyond limiting definitions of self and reconnect with your Divine self, which is always available if you are willing to love yourself out of the disempowerment you carry that's shaped by past and present experience. But it's not going to happen just by sitting down one day and deciding not to feed negativity and choosing to hope for the best – nothing real, grounded, and truly evolutionary comes from that kind of wishful thinking. You must get down in the emotional ditches and trenches of what you fear, what hurts, and what you resent and judge and hate.

Are you willing to continue forfeiting your power as a Divine, loving being by conceding to your fear or your pain? Are you going to keep leaking energy because you feel the energetic and emotional residues sourced in what's happened to you in your life? This book is intended to explain slavery (and, to a lesser extent, colonialism) from the point of view of All That Is and all of the souls involved so you can redefine why it happened and why it happened to you and your people. Remember the third and fourth truths from the opening section, combined here: *At many points along the Earth timeline, each of you has been owned and each of you has owned others.* Every single one of you has come at this issue from both sides many times, trying to figure out if this 3D, material-world dynamic in fact does, really and truly, bring you or take away power.

Are you ready to take on your many lives and the emotional debris resulting from them as creations and cocreations of souls, Divine beings learning how to be human? Are you ready to own all of your experiences as necessary for the learning journey of your soul? If so, then your identity can shift to center on the logic of soul, which vibrationally drives your life and brings experiences and opportunities to you constantly. If you insist on choosing to define yourself as disempowered because you have experienced power over/power under dynamics (as all humans have in each and every single life), then you forfeit the chance to connect with the wisdom of soul, which is taking in all of your life experiences and loving that they exist because they have taught you to be human. Slavery has happened to you and your people at many points along the Earth timeline. It has hurt, and you have felt robbed of your dignity, free will, and connection to who you have always been. It has at times caused you to lose faith in each other, humanity as a whole, God, and life and the universe. It has caused such deep pain that you have caused yourself and others destruction as you try to work out how to process the depth of the horrific experiences that have left their marks on you. It has brought you to believe life is not full of possibility and that others do not want to see you succeed. It has instilled in you a fear of trust and surrender, which are central to your nature as Divine beings living human lives learning to go from fear into love.

But what will you let these facts mean? Will you choose now to be disempowered because you were disempowered in the past? Will you continue to see yourself as a victim of your individual and collective history? Will you choose to believe that you now do not have access to the Divine power of love that is your soul's true nature because others have hurt you in the past? Are you willing to continue feeding victim/perpetrator dynamics and cycle through trying to build self-confidence on a base of anger that's a defensive response to pain?

How you choose to identify who you are is, at all times, entirely up to you.

Resolving and Releasing the Effects of Slavery

On Healing

You have now read my descriptions of what is happening from the perspective of soul when it comes to slavery and many other things. At this point, I will introduce strategies and tools for healing the effects of slavery whether you have experienced this in your current life or other lives, or if in your current life you have a genetic, ethnic, or religious energetic inheritance of the energy and effects of slavery.

To begin, I will share with you how I view healing. It is prevalent in new-age or metaphysical circles to view everyone as needing healing, and to view life as a series of things that need fixing. Beware of this trap, friends, as it comes from the linear, logical mind and is meant to focus you and keep you focused on what is wrong. It may be a central part of how you have been enculturated to see the world if you are involved in some spiritual circles, and I invite you to upgrade your view with a handful of key points.

First, you are Divine beings, which means that your true nature is as the Source of Love. You have forgotten this and so your mind takes over, wondering who you are and what's going on, what needs to be done, and how well you and others are doing those things that need to be done. Your true essence as souls is to be loving, and this is your power as a human. Instead of thinking of everything as a healing situation, look instead to how you can bring conscious awareness and intention to each situation. You can bring a loving attitude to all you encounter, seek out, and experience, and vibrating love helps you open.

Second, energetic and emotional residues stuck in your field such as the kinds I have described in this text need to leave. Bringing a loving vibration helps that happen. Consistently raising your vibration through loving intention, meditation, and choosing to release attitudes, energies, and emotions that you have carried for a long time but that no longer serve you begin a clearing process. Your intentions are Divine Commands, after all! Any issue in your life whether emotional, physical, psychological, or spiritual is the manifestation of stuck energies. For this reason, clearing is a much better word than healing.

Third, if you focus on healing, you (perhaps unintentionally) simultaneously focus on feeling sick or not being well. Realize that whatever you believe, think, and feel will manifest in the world around you and in and on your body. The physical world – including your body – will always and constantly manifest what is happening in your energetic/emotional field and consciousness (including your unconscious).

Instead of focusing on healing, focus on aligning your consciousness (doing this over time will readjust your unconscious self, too) with what matters most to and is true for you. This is to invite you instead to put your focus on being more loving, which sets healing naturally in motion without relying on your linear, logical mind to appoint itself and its fears in charge of things. Many things in your internal life will begin to organize and clean themselves up when you do this, and your external life will not be able to help following suit. *Remember always that there is nothing wrong with you, and that you are not broken.* In fact, you cannot be broken. You certainly can choose to surrender your transformative power to be loving in the face of pain and fear, but that only makes *your personality feel* broken. You as a Divine being cannot be broken! You are Goddess/God, All That Is – you are the Source of Love.

The effects of powerlessness (whether personal, cultural, racial, ethnic, or other kinds) from histories of slavery can run incredibly deep. For this reason, feelings of devastation, despair, depression, nihilism, rage, resentment, pessimism, and others can seem to threaten to take over when a person begins to address this multilife human reality in his or her emotional/energetic field. You must get grounded, connected to the Earth, and in your body fully to be able to handle these feelings. You may believe that you're supposed to control all of these negative, unattractive, destructive feelings, but instead I want you to first cultivate a serious and enduring grounding practice to enlarge and strengthen the container of your consciousness. Remember that above I described your body as a crucial tool for processing deep, intense, painful emotions from this and many other lives that may be with you now. I strongly urge you not to dive into healing slavery and its related issues before addressing your connection to your body first.

You do not need to be a weepy mess or raging maniac to heal these deep issues, but at times it may seem that you do. You may perceive that the feelings coming to the surface are too big or too devastating to deal with, and if you are not grounded, bringing these things to the surface may leave you in bed or

115

under an impromptu pillow fort for a few days or a week. *To release old emotions such as these, you must refeel them first.* You must be willing to allow them to come to the surface of conscious awareness, as up to this point they have hovered just under the surface like dark clouds, threatening to ruin everything if they were allowed to come to the surface. You cannot only talk about them and expect them to be resolved! The most talking will do (usually after some practiced self-reflection) is identify what hurts and let yourself hit the crying button so that the tears flow. You need to unearth some frightening material and you'll have to refeel that despair, rage, etc., in order to release it. Being fully in your body is the place to begin so you can handle the flow of emotions that needs to take place.

Essentially, I am describing a process not of healing but of altering and transforming your relationship with these feelings and energies within you. Often humans will wish they didn't feel a particular feeling or didn't have to feel it or, in general, so deeply or much. A truth you simply must grasp and accept if you are to make progress with any intense, deep pain, etc., is that parts of you carry these feelings and you can never, ever get rid of parts of you. You are multidimensional, meaning that you are an

116

energetic being with consciousness that exists across time. Your unconscious self is linked to all the yous associated with your soul across time, and a lot of the malfunctions you create and live through (anything that takes you away from being loving and respecting and taking care of yourself) are sourced in other-life issues stored in your unconscious that either bubble to the surface of conscious awareness or that you block from coming to the surface (and suppression always results in distortion).

As you have read this text, you may have noticed feeling at minimum stirred, perhaps a bit more as in feeling an emotion rise up to the surface. You might at times feel taken over or suddenly occupied by a feeling or memory, or the triggering of something that's always been with you but hasn't been acknowledged in an open way. This would be the start of the process. If you had such a response, reading it again may or may not elicit the same response. For some, different things will come up in each reading while for others, one theme will be stepped into in stages during subsequent rereadings. But know that you are in charge of this unearthing and resolution process. You can choose to continue the healing process by working with your body and emotions in an ongoing way, developing deeper and more fine-tuned levels of awareness about what is happening in your energetic/emotional field and learning to work more consciously and intentionally with what you experience, feel, and find within yourself.

Strategies for Resolution and Release

Humans are living on Earth so that their souls can observe what it means, costs, and is like to go from fear into love, from dealing with and being motivated by fear to being grounded in love. Slavery is, in fact, a device of All That Is for its portions to experience from both sides in order to dive or be dropped into a depth of powerlessness – which breeds fear, anxiety, and lack of trust – so that they can eventually learn to overcome it by transmuting all that pain, fear, anger, and bitterness into love.

Below I offer you three tools critical for resolving and releasing the effects and multidimensional residues of slavery. They are applicable to all deep issues that need attention and transformation, but are presented with a focus on healing the effects of slavery.

Rewriting Your History

An important element of healing the effects of slavery has been described earlier in the text, but I'd like to spell it out for you here now that you've read the bulk of my message here.

Rewriting the story about why something happened to you, others, or your ancestors is key. Always remember that the meaning of powerlessness when ascribed to painful experiences is what sets in motion and crystallizes karma, the deepest beliefs you constantly vibrate into 3D manifestation around you. Take all that is happening in your life and assume that it is in your life *only* because you need to see the vibrations you carry (especially those in your unconscious). Intentionally work to ground and release all assumptions and suspicions that what is happening in your life is so that things are harder for you, to punish you, to keep you small or unhappy, etc. As a Divine being, it is a truth that you are drawing to you through vibrational resonance all the lessons you need to learn, and those lessons center on how to go from fear into love given your particular multilife history. Look at every important person, situation, challenge, opportunity, and dynamic in your lift as part of the vibrational conspiracy of love between souls to show you how to go from fear into love, how to learn to transform fear-based motivations into love-based motivations.

This transformation is the core thread of your life story. It is why your soul is bothering to incarnate in the first place. It needs to learn, and can do so only through the lens of your consciousness, mind, heart, and life as a whole. Outside time, it's already All That Is, perfectly content in being all-loving and connected blissfully to all other souls that comprise All That Is. It desires to understand what it means, costs, looks like, and feels like to live as human, and you are executing its Divine mission by choosing to meet your life's vibrational manifestations head-on, with conscious, loving intent. Nothing could be in your life without it being part of your spiritual path! This is what I want you to focus on in order to heal the effects and results of slavery and other intense, deeply painful and angering legacies from your soul's multidimensional, multilife path.

As parts of you from all across the timeline carry pain, you will be rewriting the histories of people (other-life yous) you've never met. Begin with the feeling that comes up and takes over. Recognize that when it happens, that part of you is speaking through that emotion. It will not reason with you and present cogent arguments. It will instead well up, filling you with the intense emotion it carries and that you need to ground and work with. In that moment, you will be filled with that emotion, which could be fear, pain, anger, panic, depression, anxiety, hatred, resentment, regret, shame, guilt, or something else stressful. Prior to learning these perspectives from me, you might in these moments have believed that this fear, anger, pain, or whatever is actually you, and my explanations of your multidimensional nature will come in handy as you deal with these multidimensional emotions.

This process continues with you changing your mind about why you feel what you feel in that moment, doing so each time that energy rushes to the surface and tries to take over. *Your job is to remember that you've been shaped across the Earth timeline in many lives by real experiences, there's nothing wrong with you that you feel these things, and there's nothing with you because you believe things about your experiences, yourself, others, or the world.* But changing your mind requires holding space for this part of you to feel this pain, anger, etc., while consciously choosing to rewrite the narrative so the experience is framed in terms of all of what I have shared with you in this teaching about the intentions and vibrational power of your soul. You

121

must counsel this part of you filled with the pain, anger, etc., helping yourself to see an additional layer of interpretation about your soul's mission on top of what you are feeling. As one example, you might feel in a particular moment that something is happening to you because you deserve that it should go wrong, because maybe you assume you've done something wrong in the past and deserve failure or punishment. As you feel that, you will instead now choose to consciously see the situation that's happening as serving your growth as a soul living a human life, and you commit to seeing a higher truth (even if you don't know what that is yet specifically) as you work through the emotion.

In other words, you always honor what you feel but you upgrade the story you tell yourself about why painful experiences unfold in your life. *You change your mind about why you feel what you're feeling.* This process requires time but, more importantly, it also requires a commitment to see your life and emotions through a new lens: You are a multidimensional consciousness existing across time, and you are learning what it means that you are an energetic being and consciously operate yourself given this fact.

Releasing the Energies of Others

You may carry the energies that others have offered you, which sounds pretty benign, doesn't it? It can be, but when someone criticizes or hits you, you might take on a bit of the energy that person is sending to you. You can take on others' energy through sexual intercourse, too, including during sexual violence of any kind (or the attempt). Also, if someone thinks something about you that isn't true, you might take a bit of it on with some defensive energy, as if you have to defend yourself against what the other person thinks or says. You might also borrow or carry on someone's behalf a difficult energy when that person needs support or doesn't know how to handle or work through that energy, because you care about him or her. In short, as an energetic being you take on energy in all kinds of situations for all kinds of reasons. At this point in this teaching, I want to get specific about shedding and releasing the energies of others that you may have absorbed across time. This is an essential part of any healing process related to a deep, painful, and difficult multilife situation such as slavery.

If you have an energetic or emotional charge when you think of a person, chances are that you have carried some energy from a situation or ongoing dynamic with that person and that energy needs to go. But here, regarding healing a multidimensional past of slavery, we are speaking of the deepest sort of cache of pain, resentment, anger, disappointment, pessimism, and hatred. The energy packets you've absorbed or taken on are stored in the deepest layers of you conscious and unconscious selves.

This process rests upon changing your mind about why things happen to you, as described above. To remove others' energies in an effective and healthy way, it is imperative that you recognize them as divine beings involved in the conspiracy of love with your soul. In other words, you must see their impact upon you as part of your learning journey. In time, additionally, you must choose to be grateful for all that you have experienced, including what others have done to you.

You might still have others' energies with you because you're not aware of their presence, because you feel you deserve whatever frequency they or the situations they cocreated with you represent, or sometimes because you felt powerless in a given moment and surrendered to them and the power you believed they had over you. With the effects of slavery, everything is about the perceptions of power that the other-life yous had about self and other. Getting rid of others' energies from other lives related to all avenues involving slavery requires deciding now that you are powerful. This is about the fact that you can choose what is good for you on a daily, hourly, moment-to-moment basis, which can enable you to build the self-esteem necessary to do this process well.

Recognizing others as divine beings playing parts in your multilife story, you no longer need to feel powerless. Focus on the vibration behind and within each and every one of your choices on a day-to-day basis and you will build a foundation in the present moment that builds the kind of self-confidence that these other-life yous need to see in you in order to let go of what they carry. Consciously deciding on a regular basis that you are stronger than pain and fear, and that you are not the sum of what has happened to you or your people, creates an energetic environment in your consciousness that will help you shed the judging, shaming, negative, and abusive energies that you may be carrying from others from these other lives across the Earth timeline.

The more you intend to move beyond old and outmoded identities, the more what needs to go will come up for release. This can look like at times beings flooded with the emotions, even those heavy and un-happy ones that have followed you around your whole life and that you have at times felt you can't possibly deal with feeling, let alone working through with conscious intent. But you must decide that you are stronger than pain and fear! You must decide this constantly. Strength here is not in not feeling fear or pain, or anger or resentment or anything else challenging and damaging, but in choosing to face it. Get grounded, send cords into the Earth, breathe its energy into your body many times each day, and decide to be and remain fully in your body. To move through and release something, you cannot avoid refeeling it. I want you to adjust your view on these things to be that this is the good news! That you have to refeel is no punishment. It is a natural part of the process to come back into balance that so many call healing. And when you have moved through even just some of the past difficulty, you will feel lighter and freer, and more able to make better and right choices for yourself in the present moment and every day going forward.

You can choose to replace the image of power that guides you. Images that have come before, those based in 3D, material-world conceptions and confusions of what power is and means, can be replaced.

Daily making the right choices for yourself – those that increase self-care and self-trust – strengthens a new foundation that will make it easier and easier over time to view yourself as a divine being vibrating into your life all that you experience. That you are and have always been cocreating what happens to you based in your beliefs and interpretations means that you can now shift into a new definition of self-loving power that will naturally replace the disempowered self-images of the past due to lifetimes of slavery when it seemed that someone else was and always would be more powerful than you.

Calling Back Your Energy

The next key strategy is to call all energy that belongs to you back from across time. Know that when you feel powerless, you are perceiving that someone or something else is more powerful than you are. You might install them as important and demean yourself as not important. Living lifetimes as a slave, this may be happening constantly during those chapters of human life.

I call back all energy I may have leaked, forfeited, lost, or surrendered during lifetimes as a slave. I am ready to be whole and complete. I no longer need to learn about 3D assumptions about power through the lens of being kidnapped and forced into labor for economic gain. I no longer need to learn about power through feeling controlled, dominated, abused, raped, or killed.

And then do the opposite:

I call back all energy I may have leaked, forfeited, lost, or surrendered during lifetimes as a slave owner or overseer. I am ready to be whole and complete. I no longer need to learn about 3D assumptions about power through the lens of kidnapping and forcing others into labor for economic gain. I no longer need to learn about power through controlling, dominating, abusing, raping, or killing.

Do both sides of this process until you feel a significant overall energetic shift in how you feel in your body and how your life is going. You deserve to be whole. You deserve to have access to all of your energies in order to manage your life in conscious, healthy, intentional ways. *But only you can decide that you deserve these things. No one else, in truth, has the power to do anything to or for you.*

You are and always have been a powerful Divine energetic being, vibrating all you experience into manifestation in order to learn about what it means, looks like, and costs to be human. Heal your multilife issues stemming from the disempowerment of slavery and you will position yourself to more consciously and intentionally move from making choices based in pain and fear and move into making them from a place of peace, calm, love, and faith.

Nothing has happened to you without your soul needing you to experience it so it can grow along its evolutionary path. That slavery is such a widespread and deeply damaging human reality need no longer hurt you to the point that you forfeit your power to make the right choices for yourself at the right times and for the right reasons.

Closing

You are not what has happened to you. You are not what pain and fear you might carry from many lifetimes lived on Earth. You are not what others or you have thought of you, and you are not how others and you have treated you.

When you are ready to view all the circumstances of this life and your soul's other lives as coming up in emotion from your unconscious places, and you are ready to feel them, you can continue the evolutionary process your soul has you in this dimension to explore.

Your soul is here to learn through all manner of possible human experiences. Are you ready to embrace this? Are you ready to draw a line in the sand regarding all that has happened in your life and see it as Divine cocreations? Are you ready to own all that has come to you and bring love to how you remember and feel about it now?

Only you can decide to empower yourself with the loving, compassionate, responsible, self-respecting wisdom of soul. It is available to you always, ever present within you alongside the debris from many lifetimes of confusing, painful experience.

I know that you will heal what you carry from these many lifetimes of being on both sides of slavery. I know it because it is inevitable that you-as-humans will reach a breaking point with the victim/perpetrator paradigm so prevalent in human culture, tiring of losing and leaking energy in the face of what you have vibrated into existence as souls living human lives, ready to learn form and through all possible kinds of human dynamics.

Power comes not from who has what and who can do what to whom. Power comes from absolute, unflinching, unapologetic self-knowledge and absolute, unflinching unapologetic self-acceptance.

This text is now at an end. You are ready to dig through your emotional histories and turn pain, fear, shame, guilt, and other energy leaking emotions sourced in lifetimes involved with slavery into strength, power, and love.

Thank you for your time and energy. Take care of yourself.

Meditation: Clearing Ancestral and Individual Karma

You can read through this written meditation and take what stands out to you into a meditative, grounded, opening, clearing space,[13] or you can do the meditation as you read along. The point of it is to give you some key images and ideas to work with clearing whatever ancestral karma/beliefs you may be carrying from your family of origin in this life and personal karma/beliefs from many lives. I recommend this meditation for all, as I have stated in this teaching that you have all in many lives been on both sides of the slavery dynamic.

Another very important point of offering you this exercise is to encourage you to make self-interested, grounded, healing decisions on your own behalf. The legacy of slavery – no matter where on the globe and no matter what part of the Earth timeline – is powerlessness, and yet you are far from powerless. Any mantle of powerlessness you carry now

---

[13] See the channel's website, tdjacobs.com, for a free 13-minute grounding, heart opening, and clearing meditation I encourage all to use. Also there are a number of channeled meditation mp3s including energy work that are very useful for clearing debris and the energy of others, including ancestors.

from family/ancestry or your personal experience absolutely must be turned inside out first by working intentionally with the teachings contained in this volume thus far. Secondly, and more importantly once that is underway, you must make empowered and empowering decisions now and going forward.

Your true nature as a Divine being can shine through the lens of your human self when you adapt to certain truths about what is really happening in this dimension and in your history of human lives within it. To do this requires adapting to a higher level of interpretation of what is happening and why it is happening. That you are a Divine cocreator conspiring with other souls/people and life itself to have the experiences soul-as-you needs in order to go into fear and pain and work through them to get to love, faith, and acceptance is primary in this process. A key for you is now to see and accept that making self-interested decisions that build self-respect and -confidence is the only route to spiritual growth and human empowerment now. I intend for this meditation to show you how to approach and make such decisions so you can continually clear your energy field and consciousness/unconsciousness with love-based intent.

A note on this meditation: At some points, you might find resistance within you to doing one or more of the steps or making one or more of the included decisions. Since I've told you they are meant to empower you, you might find your mind or linear, logical self putting pressure on you to do it right. Please understand that many people have blocks and disconnections on their energy fields that may prevent some of these steps at first. The best way to work through this is to listen to the resistance and honor it. Take a step back from the process if you feel you need to. A part of you carries the resistance, fear, or block, and that part of you must be heard from for you to proceed. Listen to the feeling, thought, or belief that seems to be the source of the problem, and decide that while it's there, it's not who you are. Hear the voice of doubt, fear, or pain, and be compassionate. Accept that you've had experiences in this life and other lives that might have created barriers to feeling safe in your body or trusting of the Earth. Whatever goes on, decide it's okay, and gently persevere when the time is right. You can't do this meditation (or any other from me) wrong, and always remember that you're an energetic and emotional being learning how to more consciously operate yourself. Meditations and channeling such as this can be important tools for revealing to you what blocks you can choose to work through and release.

Meditation

Whether sitting or reclining, get comfortable. Let your breathing be easy and relaxed, but full.

Notice what's happening in your body and whatever it is, decide that it's okay. Realize that your body is always letting you know how the rest of your life is going. It cannot help but manifest the energies you're carrying, and these include beliefs, attitudes, ideas, regrets, judgments, and everything else you think and feel. Decide that you're willing to view your body as your friend, your ally. Decide that you are ready to begin a new chapter of listening and relating to it.

Send cords from the bottoms of your feet and your root or 1st chakra down into the Earth. They do not have to go far, but they could. The point is that you intentionally reach out to the Earth with your energy field, extending your consciousness beyond the limits of your physical body and inviting the energy of the Earth to join with yours.

On every inhale, welcome the energy of the Earth into your body. Draw it up into your body fully, letting it reach all parts of your body. Use it to connect all the areas of your body, using this process during each breath to outline and connect yourself as a whole being.

Do this for a handful of minutes, until your energy is calm and you feel centered in your body.

Decide: "In this moment, everything is fine and I am safe."

On each inhale until otherwise directed, put your attention on the energy coming up through your feet and root. Follow the energy coming into your feet up through your legs all the way to your root.

Repeat this decision several times, until you believe it: "In this moment, everything is fine and I am safe."

Decide: "I'm willing to be fully in my body. I'm willing to listen to my body."

Repeat this decision a handful of times, until you believe it.

Decide: "No matter what has happened to me in the past, I am willing to feel what's been stored in my body and release what does not serve me."

Decide again: "In this moment, everything is fine and I am safe."

Do this until you're sure you fully believe it.

Next, decide: "I'm willing to see all that has been in my life as serving my soul's journey." Understand that as a Divine being, you are attracting to you what you need in order to learn to go from fear into love. If you can see all that's come to you as necessary for All That Is to learn about being human, then you can get closer to empowerment.

Decide: "I'm willing to see all others in my life as serving my soul's journey."

Do this as many times as is needed either to believe it or bring up a part of self who can't agree. If the latter happens, listen to it. Make a note of why you believe it can't be true.

Decide: "I'm willing to see my family as part of the conspiracy of love my soul is involved in to learn to go from fear into love."

Decide: "I'm willing to see my family as souls behind the people, giving me many chances to learn to go from fear and pain into love and faith. I'm willing to see that we're teaching each other."

Put your attention back on the cords into the Earth and the energy of the Earth coming into your body. Trace the energy of the Earth as it moves from your feet to your root. Decide that stress and tension that's ready to go can go. Decide that the energies of other people that you have picked up and carried can go because you cannot possibly use them to tell you who you are.

Next, decide: "I'm willing to see the truth of things and surrender to a higher truth. I'm willing to let go of the pained and fearful past, let go of defenses to love, and shed resistance to seeing the truth of what my soul has laid out for me to learn to go from fear into love."

For a couple of minutes, feel the energy of the Earth coming into your body. Decide again to be in and listen to your body. Decide, "In this moment, everything is fine and I am safe."

Next, decide: "I'm willing to own all of my experiences as my Divine cocreation to learn more about going from fear into love. I'm willing to see that my soul chose my family to give me the right kinds of opportunities to go from fear into love. I'm willing to see that all that my family has experienced through the generations is part of our souls' intentions to learn to go from fear into love. I'm willing to accept that we as souls are involved in a conspiracy of love together, and I am ready to release the energies I may have absorbed from and carried on behalf of them.

"I'm willing to accept that I was born into that family for a reason, and I'm ready to leave behind the heavy, damaging, and pained energies that might have been floating around my family system for generations. I accept that all souls when human do all they can to learn to go from fear and pain into love and faith, and I accept that we're all works in progress. I'm ready to release all of the debris my family and ancestors handed me in the spirit of giving me an idea of how to be human and deal with emotion and energy."

Thank your parents, any siblings you have, your grandparents and other relatives (even if you knew them very little or not at all) for agreeing as souls to bring your human self into the world. Thank them for giving you a model of how to be human. With this gratitude, decide you are no longer willing to carry their energies. Decide, "I am a Divine being who is a work in progress, learning how to be human as I go. I'm ready to make my own decisions for my own reasons and on my own terms. I'm ready to honestly evaluate more and better choices based in self-respect and self-care. I honor the contracts my soul has with family in this life and other lives, and I release myself across time from any obligation to carry forward any energy or emotion from my people."

At this point, open your crown or 7th chakra (on top of your head) and breathe in from the Earth and through the crown simultaneously. Bring each energy to your heart or 4th chakra (the center of your chest). For a couple of minutes, relax on your exhales.

Then breathe out through root and crown on each exhale. In from each source on the inhales, out through both sources on the exhales. Do this until further notice.

Decide: "I'm ready to release myself across time of the perceived need to carry the energies of others, including ancestral karmic inheritance. I surrender these energies to the Earth with gratitude for my ancestors for offering me a model of being human, and with gratitude to the Earth for willingly receiving these energies I can no longer use to grow along my path.

"I forgive myself across time for carrying others' energies and emotions. I release myself across time from any real or perceived vow, promise, and obligation to carry the karmic pain and confusion of others, including my families in many lives.

"I call back to myself from across time any and all energies forfeited, lost, leaked, and loaned to others both in family and all other relationships. I am ready to be whole and complete.

"I forgive myself across time for causing myself and others pain. I forgive all others across time for causing me pain. I'm willing to accept that we're inextricably linked across time in a vast and complex conspiracy of love so that we all may have many opportunities to learn to go from fear into love."

Next, take the energy you are breathing in through your root and crown and breathe it out through your heart or 4th chakra. On every exhale, relax open and breathe out through this heart center. Notice if you have tension that prevents this. If you do, decide, "In this moment, I'm safe enough to relax in order to release and move on."

Exhaling through your heart, decide: "I'm ready to heal all disempowerment from the karmic past by making better choices: All of my choices are based in self-respect and lead to self-care. I own my power to make the right choices for the right reasons and at the right times. I'm willing to listen to my body and trust my gut instinct. I'm willing to become the source of love for myself. All of my choices are based in self-respect and lead to self-care."

Repeat the last two lines as many times as you need to in order to believe that you have the power to respect and care for yourself. Along the way, listen to and acknowledge any parts of you that resist this truth, noting any negative emotion, thought, or belief and always remember that you are not that resistance; you are a Divine being living as a human, a

Divine work in progress learning over lifetimes to go from fear into love.

Decide: "All debris related to my many lifetimes on Earth that holds me back or makes me feel small can go down into the Earth, and I thank the Earth for receiving it. I choose to release all debris I carry from my family system and ancestors in this life and many lives all across the Earth timeline, and that energy can go into the Earth, as well."

Take your time in this space. Revisit anything in the meditation that gave you pause or over which you might have stumbled or by which were surprised. When you're ready to come of this meditative space, go slow and realize that deep shifts might have begun for you during this process. If so, notice over the next few days what's happening in your energy field, emotions, and physical body. It's normal for the physical body to adjust in various ways following this kind of meditation. Listen to your body and treat it as an ally as it tells you how your emotions, thoughts, beliefs, and clearing are going.

Thank you, and take care of yourself.

About Djehuty

Djehuty (a.k.a. Thoth, St. Germain, and Merlin) is an ascended master. He has been made a mythological and/or deified figure in all Earth cultures. He represents the Hermes archetype: translator, teacher, scribe, and mediator. His commitment is to serve humanity by teaching humans how to evolve and move toward the evolutionary goal of the manifestation experiment: Learning in human form to remember their divine nature as the source of love.

About the Channel

Tom Jacobs is an Evolutionary Astrologer and Channel. A graduate of Evolutionary Astrologer Steven Forrest's Apprenticeship Program, Tom has a global practice of readings, coaching, and tutoring to help people understand what they came to Earth to do and supporting them in making it happen. He is the author or channel of 16 books on astrology, mythology, and spirituality and original astrological natal reports on Lilith and 2012 & emotional healing. Tom also energetically programs a variety of stones and crystals to interrupt old patterns and support you in making better choices and living a healthier, happier life.

Contact Tom via http://tdjacobs.com.

By Tom Jacobs

Channeled Books
Approaching Love
Understanding Loss and Death
Goddess Past, Present, and Future
Conscious Revolution: Tools for 2012 and Beyond
Djehuty Speaks (a collection of the above 4 titles)
Conscious Living, Conscious Dying

Astrology, Mythology, and Spirituality Books
The Soul's Journey I: Astrology, Reincarnation, and Karma with a Medium and Channel
The Soul's Journey II: Emotional Archaeology
The Soul's Journey III: A Case Study
Lilith: Healing the Wild
Chiron, 2012, and the Aquarian Age: The Key and How to Use It
Saturn Returns: Thinking Astrologically
Living Myth: Exploring Archetypal Journeys
Seeing Through Spiritual Eyes: A Memoir of Intuitive Awakening
Pluto's 2012 Retrograde and the First Square to Uranus in Aries (ebook only)

Natal Reports
The True Black Moon Lilith Natal Report
Living in the Present Tense Emotional Healing Natal Report

Made in the USA
Monee, IL
19 September 2021